A
Pear
for the
Teacher

With happy memories!
Daisy M. Styles
4301-17 St. N.E.
Tuscaloosa, al.
35404
May 24, 1973

Daisy M. Styles

553-9693

sevgo press ● *northport, alabama*

A
Pear
for the
Teacher

Contents

Dedicated to the Memory of

DR. JASPER E. HARVEY

One of the greatest privileges of my life was to have been associated with Dr. Jasper E. Harvey during all of his ten years in Alabama and to have maintained that friendship throughout the remaining years of his life. My first association with Dr. Harvey was as a student, then as a departmental instructor with him as chairman, and, of course, always as a cherished friend. He was not only one of the greatest teachers of our time, but a loving family man as well. As an administrator, he never lost the "common touch." His understanding of people was unmatched. He always told his classes that it is not so important what we do *for* children as what we do *to* them.

Preface

The title of this book was chosen eighteen years ago at a rural school in Alabama when a little boy brought to this teacher, not the traditional apple, but a sack full of pears — the best gift he had to offer. *A Pear for the Teacher* is written in order to help the parents and teachers of exceptional children, and perhaps the children themselves, see how others in similar circumstances have handled their often particularly difficult situations. This book was made possible from responses to letters sent to pupils and parents which said, "After ten years of retirement, I have given myself the goal of pulling together from my files some of the information which helped me so much in my work, and, hopefully, might help others." I now thank them for the most important parts of *A Pear for the Teacher*.

The stories included in the present volume represent every possible exceptionality: Those children who are emotionally disturbed or socially maladjusted, the mentally retarded and the physically handicapped, the gifted, the communication-disordered, and the learning disabled. Even "normal" children are represented. These narratives were written by family members, or dictated—sometimes by the children themselves—to the author. Some of the people described were never actually my pupils, but our paths crossed in various ways. Many others could have been included, but, unfortunately, choices had to be made because of space limitations; however, an attempt was made to include all of the original members of my first special class at Cottondale School in Tuscaloosa, Alabama, in 1957.

The essential contents of letters from others included herein were not changed, though they were edited somewhat for clarity and expression. However, the sharing of those communications does not necessarily imply that I agree with every single action depicted, though I certainly understand the thoughts and emotions that are expressed. In *A Pear for the Teacher,* one will see displayed the whole range of human emotions and will be told first hand of the confusion, the fear, the false hopes, the guilt and even suicidal despair experienced by those afflicted with some disability or abnormality and by those persons who—either through familial love or humane and professional obligation—dedicate their lives to relieving that suffering.

The reader will witness extreme dissatisfaction with doctors, teachers, and entire school systems, and will hear—almost in the same breath—extravagant and heartfelt praise for those in authority. Alongside the parents, the teachers, and, most especially, the children, the reader will join the tortured search for answers, and will experience both the crushing failures and the successes far beyond expectation, the terrible heartaches and the joys beyond measure.

Acknowledgements

A debt of gratitude is due so many that I am sure to leave some out. To a school system which made teaching "fun;" to the University of Maryland Child Study Institute which impressed upon its participants the importance of those being taught as well as materials and methods and gave instructions for in-depth study as well as objective methods for doing this through anecdotal techniques; to good teachers through the years who taught by example as well as subject matter and so were able to inspire others to become teachers; to the many parents and former pupils, as well as acquaintances, who so willingly shared their educational experiences and life stories in order to help me in taking inventory of my small part in the educational process; to many former students and colleagues who supplied anecdotes. To Dr. Raymond Elliott, chairman of the Department of Special Education, University of Alabama, who gave time and encouragement as well as the help of his administrative assistant, Sharon Thompson in coordinating the typing, done largely by Carol Poole; to Emil Kunze in the Graphics area of the Educational Media Department who proofed all my old reel tapes to determine their usability and unearthed some gems; to George Gordon of University Legal Services who provided my legal permission forms; to Dean Roth who suggested John Seymour as a possible publisher; to Dr. M. L. Roberts who was never too busy to listen to my questions and kept me moving ahead.

To Dr. Alyene Reese who proofed the manuscript for medical inaccuracies; to Kathryn, Laurel, and Leigh Harvey who provided me with the background information on Jasper; to Dr. Judy Smith-Davis, at that time president-elect of the teacher education division, for Bureau of Education for the Handicapped, Washington, D.C. who gave permission to use the tribute she had written and published in memory of Dr. Harvey; to Myra Grady, Allene and Tommy Russell who were the first to read early chapters and encouraged me to proceed; To Dr. Bobby Palk, the only person to read the entire manuscript prior to editing and suggested the one change from a serious outline to one in keeping with the Pear; to Bill who gave me the title twenty-five years before the book was written.

To my beloved Latin and English teacher, Miss Eltie Haynie, of 54 years back, who did my proofing for grammatical errors from Tyson Manor Nursing Home in Montgomery; to my three children who gave me anecodotes without knowing it; and to Ben and the Alberta Baptist Church who allowed him to do most of my duplicating while he served them as a staff member; finally to George who put up with me though two years of unknown hours of typing, writing and sorting with a patient and understanding feeling of pride which those of you who know him recognize as the nature of George H. Styles. Acknowledgments do not seem to be complete without a word of thanks to my God who has helped me to retain reasonably good mental and physical health these twelve years into retirement so that I might bring this project to completion.

Daisy M. Styles

Foreword

The stories special education teachers could tell would fill a book. Daisy Styles has filled such a book at just the right time to remind us of what special education is all about—the joys, the humor and the bittersweet days of teaching exceptional children.

Thirty years ago when people were beginning to think about starting up special education programs statewide there were already a few teachers who were interested in getting into this new field. One of these was Daisy Styles. At first there was a notion that special education might not last very long because not many people would want to teach "those" children. Daisy believed things would work out, and she has seen special education not only last, but grow dramatically as teachers came into the field because of those children.

Daisy Styles has dedicated this book to Jasper Harvey. He was one of the first persons actually to have studied special education in a new program at the University of Texas. He had the awesome task of inventing a field as he went along. His strength and force of character pulled special education together in Alabama. Soon there were teachers arriving in Tuscaloosa to study everything they could about how to work with exceptional children. Jasper needed someone to assist him with the teacher education program, and first among the Alabamians he asked to join the faculty at the University was Daisy Styles. Daisy taught the methods courses and worked as a liaison person with the schools—placing, supervising and instructing student teachers. Daisy and Jasper became a team and together they laid the foundation for teacher training in special education in Alabama.

Many students at the University of Alabama studied special education. The names of those who are teachers, administrators, professors, psychologists, and advocates for exceptional children would fill another book. Not only students in education, but students in business, psychology, home economics, and social work, and some very notable members of the Crimson Tide football team had courses in this field. Even the publisher of this book, John Seymour, was a student of Jasper Harvey.

In the 10 years that Jasper and the 13 years that Daisy were at Alabama there was the beginning of a deep spirit of caring about what is right and good for exceptional people. This spirit continues to ripple out into every stream of Alabama life today. Those of us who are members of the special education family of Alabama have a heritage of belief, commitment, and toughmindedness in overcoming difficult times. When people talk about all the problems and issues in education today, it would be well to call their attention to *A Pear for the Teacher*. It puts everything back into proper focus.

Gale Lambright, Chairperson
Program for Gifted Children
University of South Alabama

Chapter One

THE FRUIT

"Children are like wet cement. Whatever falls on them makes an impression."

- Hoim Ginott

Statistics indicate that in every first grade class there can be found at least one exceptional child, with the figure in most states hovering between 2.5 to 4.0%. This fact seems to be so difficult for many people—parents, teachers, administrators, and the public—to comprehend, and this unfortunate and often damaging ignorance is revealed in statement after statement made every day.

I was once asked, by a prominent citizen, "Where do all those retarded you work with come from?" "Six of the ones in my current class are from your neighborhood," I replied. I was told by the principal of a school where the formation of a special class was being considered that, "We just don't have that caliber of child in our school." After biting my tongue and counting to ten during a period of dead silence, I said, "Handicapping conditions are no respecter of persons." It turned out that the sons and daughters of preachers, university professors, lawyers, doctors, doctoral candidates, and teachers were among those screened for the class.

"We don't need a special education unit at our school because we are not in an economically deprived area," stated another principal. "That is not the deciding factor in special education," I said, "though it can and does contribute." Two years later, efforts had to be made to eliminate the overflow of students who could not be accommodated by the special unit which had been created at that school. This enormous demand provided further evidence that exceptional children often need the security of a special class in order to avoid, or at least combat, the pressure to achieve beyond their limits. Special attention is required to help them over the hurdle of emotional instability, and to aid them in dealing with the problems of learning disorders or disabilities, mental retardation, social maladjustment, or physical handicaps.

A typical day which illustrates the ubiquitiousness of exceptionalities was that of the first class meeting of the 1967 fall term student teachers and interns, a day the events of which could have convinced even a hardened cynic of the value and efficacy of special education. During the brief drive from an urban school to the state university, I noticed a girl from a state institution for severely handicapped children, dressed neatly in a white uniform, walking briskly and happily along her way to a local cafeteria, where she worked and supported herself under the supervision of Vocational Rehabilitation Services.

I also observed a young man pushing a lawn mower to his place of work, a young man who maintained what must have been quite a thriving business by cutting grass on most spring, summer, and fall days. Known to live at home with his parents, he later successfully maintained that home alone. In the winter he could be seen picking up cans and bottles along the roads, taking much more pride in his community than most of us! It was clear, by the way, that there were certain other important lessons that he had learned quite well. One day I stopped to offer him a ride when it was raining; he thanked me, but declined, "I'm sorry, but I must not ride with stangers."

Upon visiting a special class—in order to make plans for a student teacher—I noted that the school principal himself was handicapped; he wore a leg-brace and walked with a limp caused by a shrapnel wound during military service. The school custodian was unusually small, and it took a second look to determine that he was indeed an adult. "He's a mighty good janitor," the principal remarked.

Encounters with some of the students at this particular school could only serve to further strengthen and confirm one's feeling about the value of special education as it served critical needs of children. I recommended that a fourth-grade girl undergo a hearing evaluation after a private interview during which she had constantly strained to hear and had watched lip movements very closely. One particular child in the class for educable mentally retarded, pointed out to me in the lunchroom, already had an ulcer and was known to be very easily upset.

Even after I left school that day in 1967, these encounters continued. I noticed a pre-school age boy wearing glasses with very thick lenses and straining desperately to see an airplane. Upon arriving at a shopping center, where I hoped to find a gift for my three-year old granddaughter, I saw a man I knew who had learning difficulties, but who could install electrical wiring when given the chance to do so. Shopping hurriedly, I found a book for my granddaughter, a book which I barely scanned before purchasing it. I later realized that this book could very easily have served as a special education text, with its message that all little girls are different...except at the end of the day when they all need a lap to sit on! At 7:00 p.m. that same day, I attended the wedding of a young lady who had been a member of my Sunday School class. This woman had grown up without parents, and—except for the loving care of her aunt and uncle—might very well have found herself labeled as "emotionally disturbed." At 8:00 p.m., I capped off a very full day by attending another wedding, this time involving a close friend of my son, a boy who had once been one of my fourth grade pupils. Despite having spent a full semester of that fourth-grade year in bed because of rheumatic fever, and with little homebound instruction, this young man had distinguished himself in his high scholastic achievement. He had gone on to earn a degree in electrical engineering in a year less than many students require.

All of these incidents, combined with having met a new group of student teachers who were very gifted—as have been all of those student teachers in Special Education through the years—made the day complete, and convinced me that there existed a remarkably high percentage of exceptional people in the community.

Bill

"To handle yourself, use your head; to handle others, use your heart."
- The English Digest

It had been another one of those summers! The fruit had been so abundant that my two teenage children, my husband and I had worked late, night after night, even on Labor Day weekend, peeling pears and running them through the food chopper to make relish, putting up those final jars of preserves and pineapple-pear honey, canning halves for salad, and even baking some. The first day of school was a welcome relief—as it always was, for over thirty years—from a busy though wonderful summer filled to the brim with enjoyment as a result of life with my green-thumbed husband, George, an enthusiastic farmer and teacher. He felt sure that it was I who finally cursed the fig tree in the backyard and who encouraged blight on the apple, plum, and peach trees. Little did I realize what it would be like when he could devote all of his time to those pursuits in ten years of retirement!

On that first day of school, Tuesday after Labor Day, a student named Bill arrived, carrying a grocery bag that was so heavy, so full of something, that barely had he been able to manage it on the crowded school bus. A smile stretching from ear to ear indicated that the child had brought a gift for his teacher of the previous year. I was that teacher, and I realized that Bill was not trying to be an "apple polisher," but rather wished to make a genuine gesture of love and respect. That moment was probably among the most difficult I ever had to face in my teaching career. I felt somewhat like the child who was asked to return thanks to the Lord for a family meal, and who—after all heads were bowed—had hesitated, then asked his mother, "How can you be thankful for liver?" You see, Bill had brought me another bag of pears!

I felt that it was important to accept the boy's gift in the spirit in which it was offered. Many of my university professors had impressed one crucial fact on me, that you begin to teach when you realize the worth of each child, when you are able to emphasize the positive rather than the negative, and when you have built a real appreciation for and rapport with each child. I tried to genuinely thank him for his gift, knowing full well that my family would throw me out of the house when I suggested another night of peeling pears.

Yes, that sack of pears was truly a special offering, and likely was the first thing Bill had ever brought to a teacher, though he had often sat and watched in silence as the gifts of other students were "oohed" and "aahed" over. Since no fruit was ever growing at Christmas or at the end of school, there had never been anything to give. Most often, in fact, there was probably not even enough to eat at home. This gift came from a child who slept, with no sheets and a few tattered quilts, on a couch which bore his every curve, and who had only his dog to keep him warm. He wore his clothes hard and long, until they literally fell to pieces or were simply outgrown; he slept in them, then wore them to school day after day.

This indeed was a gift that meant something! I knew these things about Bill's home because my husband-principal had seen to it that I visited the homes of my students, and had come along with me as well. The Tuscaloosa County Board of Education even provided half-holidays the first week of school for this purpose. How could my husband find time for such excursions while school registers had to be completed, materials ordered, and lesson plans made? Well, those tasks could wait! How did we ever get so busy teaching that we lost time for learning things that would make our teaching so much more meaningful and practical?

By the way, I suppose I should mention that the story of the pears is not quite complete, not without a mention of the events of the second day of school after Labor Day. A number of my students, following Bill's example, brought me gifts. What did they bring? You guessed it . . . more sacks of pears! I now wished that I had not been so grateful the day before.

I once remarked to someone that the only time I had ever been able to speak publicly was on the night of my high school graduation fifty years eariler. In the audience was a certain young man who was known to have come only for my graduation. That young man was George, and he carried a gift—not pears, but a white purse. "Whatever I did, I overdid—she hasn't stopped talking since!" he said later.

After receiving that massive influx of pears, our family had no shortage of canned pears, and had no need to even plant another tree until 1980. Now, in retirement, we finally have one bearing, with a grafted limb of every variety known to Hastings. We even discovered in 1984 that dried pears are fantastic, when eaten as a tidbit or when prepared like any other dried fruit. Oh, to have known that some years earlier! But as my smart principal often remarked, "We learn most of what we do after it can no longer do us any good or far too early." The ways in which we attempt to teach and bring up children are good demonstrations of this maxim.

I suppose that I appreciated Bill's gift to me as much as any other I received during my teaching career. I cannot really recall many gifts during the years so readily—except for those which have been carefully preserved, and I, despite a failing memory, still know who gave me each one. Of the perishable gifts, Bill's will never be forgotten. It represented the best he had to bring, it came at a very unexpected time, it was given from the heart, and he knew that it was useful. How many teachers ever got a first-day-of-school present?

That is what teaching is all about: to bring out the best in each child, to accept what he can do without comparing him with others, and to make him feel proud of his accomplishments. To Bill, and to the fourteen students in that first class for Educable Mentally Retarded, I offer sincere thanks for allowing me to know you. My sincere gratitude is yours for the privilege of learning far more from you than I ever taught. George often wondered if I ever taught you anything because I used all my time learning from you. It was wonderful to grow together as we spent those five years in each other's company.

Johnny

The first crippled child in any of my classes was Johnny, a delightful fifth grader on crutches who had extremely curved legs as a result of a spinal injury suffered when he was two years old. He had fallen from the fender of a pick-up truck driven by his father and been run over, his dad having been unaware that the boy was had fallen from the fender of a pick-up truck driven by his father and been run over, his dad having been unaware that the boy was anywhere near the truck. In spite of his injury, Johnny never expected any favors; his mother encouraged him in this attitude by treating him no differently than his three brothers and sister. Just as much housework was expected of him as of the others, and I can still picture him hoeing in the garden when I made one of my home visits. He even played softball at school, though someone else would run the bases for him.

My special interest in Johnny was heightened after my husband George and I, along with a number of other local school teachers, chose to participate in a four-year inservice course from Dr. Daniel Prescott's Child Study Institute at the University of Maryland. A part of our assignment was to select one pupil from our class on which to do an in-depth case study involving an extensive anecdotal record. I chose Johnny's younger brother, a quiet, studious little boy named Bobby Joe. (Who will know only now that his case study was used in other workshops all over the United States after the University of Maryland gave permission to release the information.)

We compiled a wealth of information concerning Johnny's family and the warm and loving atmosphere of their household, and by this effort we really got to know Johnny. In addition to Bobby Joe, Johnny had a baby sister, Imogene, and an older brother, James. Their dad was employed at a municipal waterworks. Quite often the other family members spoke of the love they felt for Johnny, who would undergo spinal surgery while in high school.

Studies like this one helped to increase interest in this aspect of a "handicapped(?)" person's life, especially later when the field of special education became a chosen profession.

In the following letter, we read Johnny's account of his life history:

Dear Mrs. Styles:

As I told you on the phone, probably the thing that influenced my life more than anything else was my parents and their attitude toward me. Basically, they treated me the same as my brothers and sister. They taught me to do things for myself, instead of doing them for me. I also had to do my share of the chores. Don't get me wrong; there were things that I could not do. They recognized this and substituted other chores for these.

My parents also allowed me to reach out and do things for myself that, looking back, I know scared them to death. For example, I remember several times when kids would be playing in the trees in the backyard. I would climb up to be with them. My mother tells me now how much it scared her. Also, I know it scared them for me to learn to drive the tractor and, later, to start driving the car. The point is that they allowed me to do so while they cautiously stood by. Doing things for myself and taking care of myself allowed me to move away from home upon graduation from college, and not be dependent.

It was 1951 when I entered your fifth grade class. I was eleven at that time. It was about then that the special school for the handicapped was opened at Northington, but we decided that public school would be better for me since I did not have a particular problem with it. Now I know that was a good decision in preparing me to deal with society.

To give you a brief summary of my life, I graduated from high school in 1960, and started the state university in the fall. I am not sure when I decided to go to college, or if I ever did. As far back as I can remember, it was assumed that I would attend college. I chose electrical engineering because engineers were in great demand at the time, and it looked interesting. To tell the truth when I graduated from high school, I knew very little about what an engineer did.

Upon graduation in January of 1965, I went to work for a large corporate firm which was deeply involved in the space program. In my 20 years with that firm, I have worked on several interesting and exciting programs. I worked on the cabling and communication systems for the Saturn V launch vehicles which carried men to the moon, as a radar analyst on a major missile system, as a system analyst on Spacelab (a space laboratory built in Europe and launched by the U.S.). I am currently a staff engineer working with computer software developement in the Southeast. During this period, I have been fortunate to have witnessed a Saturn V launch and two Space Shuttle launches from Cape Kennedy, Florida, and several missile launches at White Sands, New Mexico.

Now let me tell you about the best part of my life, my family. I met my wife in 1969 at a party and we dated for almost a year before we were married in February, 1970. We have two boys, ages 14 and 12.

Looking back over my past, while I am writing this, makes me realize that I was lucky to have the teachers which I had. You always allowed me to do things my way until I asked for help, then you were always there to help. I wonder how many trays I spilled while learning to carry a lunch tray? By the way, I still carry my own tray in the cafeteria at work.

I hope this will be of help to you in preparing your book, and if there are any specifics that you need, let me know. Feel free to use as little or as much as you need of this to get your points across. Good luck on your efforts.

Sincerely,
Johnny

Billy

Born on December 19, 1942, Billy was the second son of a mother who was a graduate nurse, and of a father who made concrete blocks and worked as a plasterer. His older brother, a "normal boy," was born on March 29, 1940. Billy's mother served as a private duty nurse, and worked at various hospitals, including a rural county hospital—where she was employed for seventeen years—and the Student Health Center at a nearby university.

When Billy was two, his father was killed in a single—vehicle truck accident when the heavy load of furniture he was transporting apparently shifted. My interview with the family took place in the beautiful tan, brick home on February 16, 1985, the fortieth anniversary of the father's death. Following the accident, Billy's mother had recieved $43.00 per month in Social Security benefits for herself and her two sons; later, she entered the home construction business in order to supplement their income and to be at home with her boys more than full-time nursing might have allowed.

At birth, Billy was jaundiced and slept most of the time. It was later determined that there had been an Rh incompatability, although no blood transfusion had been done; at 18 months of age Billy was taken to a clinic in a nearby metropolitan center, and the doctor who examined him was appalled that his condition had not been determined at birth and attempts made at correction. He was diagnosed as spastic cerebral palsied. He walked at age four; his verbal communication was largely a matter of making signs. His mother, brother, and other relatives from a closeknit family treated him like a normal child, and he was never petted or spoiled because of his exceptionalities.

Billy entered first grade at the age of six years, nine months. Before long it was discovered that he had a hearing loss, and was fitted with a hearing aid to which he never adjusted; "It made me very nervous," he said. He spent two years in regular classes before being transferred to one for the physically handicapped. He remained there until age twelve during which time he met a "fantastic" teacher, Mrs. Harwood. He had several teachers, but it was a sad day when Mrs. Harwood moved to California.

Billy's mother remarried. They moved to a farm where Billy loved the work and even drove a tractor—which later made it easier for him to teach himself to drive a car. Though the step—father had excellent rapport with Billy, the marriage failed.

In 1955 his mother built a house in town where Billy, at the age of fourteen, was enrolled in his school's first special class which was taught by Mrs. Margaret Perritt who had a degree in Speech Pathology.

Billy became my student in the fall of 1957. I was coming from my one and only year of first grade teaching, which was preceded by two years experience in seventh grade, and fourteen years at the fourth and fifth grade levels. It was with mixed emotions that I chose to try the Special Class after my husband had so eagerly applied for and was successful the preceeding January in establishing a class in our school as one of the system's first two units.

A summer of audited courses relieved my anxiety and ignorance to a degree. Always, I had felt—that with many of my pupils—how wonderful it would have been to have had a little more time for individual attention or to move at a slower pace and this seemed a possibility with a smaller class. I knew the pupils enrolled in that first special class already. I had been intrigued by their smiles and changed attitudes evident after their being a part of that class for one semester. Whereas many had been "bottom rung" in regular class, they had exhibited so much more self-confidence and Mrs. Perritt had seen to it that they were very much a part of school. I had observed that Billy, the oldest, was their "leader" and how he loved all his buddies. This fact made it easier for me to make the move to "special" education at mid-point in my teaching career. I never regretted the move and came to appreciate greatly the fact that many exceptional people exert far more effort to achieve to their limit than most of the ordinary people are willing to do.

But let us return to Billy. He had slight scoliosis, poor but understandable speech, and some athetoid movements along with his spasticity. Billy showed a keen interest in everything but had not learned to read more than a few sight words even by age 15, and this problem persists for him today—even after attendance in adult classes. Although writing was difficult for him, he did enjoy arithmetic, and he had no behavioral problems. He attended church with his mother, and he was one of the most well—adjusted teenagers possible, with a delightful sense of humor.

Two incidents in my association with Billy stand out vividly, one involving an injury he suffered while skating on the amphitheater floor built for the school by the Civitans. Skating was open to students of all ages, but Billy was the only child from the special class to choose it as a physical education activity—perhaps because it allowed him to associate with the older children. Miss Susie, a substitute teacher who later became the school secretary, was present the day Billy was injured when he fell on the concrete, and an ambulance had to be called to take him to the hospital. His recuperation was very painful, with athetoid movements increased by stress; a pin was placed in his broken leg and removed surgically several years later. His mother, the nurse, lovingly said, "Billy, you will just have to take some of the pain as you will have a worse problem if I give you enough pain shots to relieve it all." The other kids at school were very upset over Billy's plight, and the class made get-well cards—even visiting as a group after he came home.

During this period he made for himself the cutest trinket box complete with a tiny lock and key.

When Billy returned to school, he came with his skates, but he did not intend to use them; he asked, "Who wants my skates?" I witnessed all this with mixed feelings, but I felt good that Billy had faced one of the realities of his life without seeming to be depressed and was able to go on happily to other pursuits. Realistic goals are very wise for all of us.

Another important event in Billy's life was when he became aware of the possibility of driving a car, a subject that is sure to come up when a boy nears the age of sixteen. I will never forget the gleam in his eyes as he asked, "Do you mean they will let me drive?" I answered in the affirmative, but it occurred to me that his mother would not be very happy when he got home with the news. She must have shuddered at the thought of Billy behind the wheel of a car. Billy did get a license eleven years later through the intercession of a neighbor, who persuaded the family and people at the driver's license office to allow Billy to take an oral test. His step-father bought him a small English car, and he has since driven everywhere with no special adaptations. He loves to go to Florida for fishing trips, and he has had only one ticket—in a large city for exceeding the speed limit.

Two years after their entering my class, I took Billy and the other two sixteen-year-old boys in the class—Carl and Bill—to to a Vocational Rehabilitation Evaluation Center for testing, sure that they would all pass with flying colors, but they were turned down and further schooling was recommended. "What schooling?" I wondered, since there were no high school special education classes available in our community at that time.

Graduation day came at the elementary school, and I'll never forget the picture that was taken of Carl, Bill, Billy, and me. They stood on stage with the sixth graders, handsome and proud in their white shirts and ties—items which I suspect Billy had provided for the other two. My memories of that happy occasion are particularly poignant when I consider the difficulties encountered by the three boys, and especially by Billy, following their graduation and subsequent enrollment in junior high.

Billy endured the seventh grade for two years, with Carl and Bill not even lasting one, and it was a sad day for Billy when he was informed that there was no use in his returning to school the next year. Oh, if only our high school special education teachers had entered the picture a year or so earlier than they did! "No more schooling for me," Billy resolved, after receiving his final failing report card, and even now—in his early forties— the word "school" turns Billy off. I would feel the same way if I had been through what he had, and I realize that it must have been very difficult for him to be eighteen and have no real way to get an education, to find girls to date and work to do, or to associate with his peers.

Billy was able to continue his schooling when a federal grant sponsored jointly by VRS and SPE, under the supervision of Dr. Harvey, established one of eleven Research and Demonstration classes for Alabama in our community. The class was located down by the railroad tracks in an old warehouse, and Billy was one of the seven lucky ones enrolled, and he had a fine teacher for three years and an outstanding shop instructor. It was a good experience all the way around for Billy, who did quite well at furniture refinishing.

After finishing his education once and for all, Billy has worked job after job, often under difficult and physically debilitating conditions, and almost invariably for minimum wage or less. Billy worked in a service station for six years, filling cars with gasoline and handling money, and—though his wage was one dollar per day—was always smiling, well-dressed, and carefully groomed. He packaged baby chicks for seven years, earning $3.25 an hour, until the constant standing on wet concrete floors in all kinds of weather aggravated his arthritis.

At 29, Billy married a girl ten years his junior, but the marriage lasted only one month. Perhaps she felt she was missing out on much of the joy of being young. Billy's mother had built the young couple a small house, and Billy lived alone there after the breakup until he found it impossible to maintain the place and pay utilities. Billy moved back home, as he would again some time later, after his mother had built him another small house near hers.

After moving to a coastal city to live with his brother, Billy found a job in the laundry room of a Hilton Hotel—where he learned to operate all the heavy equipement—but the continual handling of heavy loads of wet sheets again brought on back trouble and he had to quit. The hotel, however, gave Billy a great letter of recommendation citing his perfect attendance on the job as well as his outstanding productivity as an employee. Upon his return home after seven months, Billy and his mother were convinced that he had best look into disability coverage, and he currently draws a Social Security check of $380.00 per month, based on his deceased father's income. We also have determined, after various inquiries, that Billy can work some and still retain his eligibility for total disability.

The spring of 1985 saw Billy making various attempts to get work, attempts which failed to bear fruit. At the close of the initial interview in February, I asked Billy, "What would you most like at this stage in your life?" His very quick answer was, "to have a job."

The story does not end there, however. Billy now has a worthwhile job and performs it admirably. This turn of events is particularly fortuitous at the present time for Billy, because his mother fell and required cerebral surgery. Bill handled all the hospital bills, visited daily in the hospital for three months, and now sees to the house and takes care of his wheelchair-bound mother.

Wayne

Wayne was born in 1942, weighing six pounds, nine ounces. His mother had German measles during this, her first pregnancy, and also suffered a serious fall down some steps. At the age of six months, Wayne began having petit mal seizures. Wayne would eventually have two younger brothers and one sister; his father was a welder and preacher who died when Wayne was eighteen years old. At the age of six Wayne enrolled in school at Children's Center—where I saw him from time to time—and stayed for six or seven years.

When his father came to our community to work, Wayne enrolled in our special school in an old army hospital barracks, with an exceptional teacher. Wayne's reading skills at this point were at about a third grade level, and he did arithmetic at a fifth grade level.

At age fifteen, he enrolled at the Research and Demonstration (R&D) Center workshop and class with a beloved teacher, who became an important state leader. Wayne remained in the workshop for two years after the Research class project was complete, and then looked for jobs everywhere without success. It was also during this period that his father died and his mother later remarried.

Under the supervision of Vocational Rehabilitation, Wayne worked at the sheltered workshop from 7:00 a.m. to 3:30 p.m., then worked at a convenience store until 11:00 p.m. Even with his curved legs and slow gait, he walked home every night from the store, though the van provided by Vocational Rehabilitation transported him from the workshop to the store and picked him up at home every morning at 5:00. He later worked as a janitor at his stepfather's garage for twenty dollars a week and room and board. Wayne has a sister who is a nurse and his youngest brother works on oil rigs in Texas—usually only coming home for Christmas. Another brother has been institutionalized since the age of ten with much worse seizures than Wayne.

Wayne endured a rather trying period of unemployment and retraining in the mid-to-late-1970's before securing a full-time position as a custodian at a local Baptist church in 1979. In addition to that church a nearby recreation center had an opening for an extra janitor, and Wayne was allowed to take the job on a trial basis. During the spring of 1985, while I was trying to help Billy find work, we stopped to see Wayne at the church— thereby allowing the two former classmates to renew an old friendship—and I was tremendously impressed by the encouragement that Wayne offered Billy. I wish that I had a tape of that conversation, because no rehab counselor or university professor could have sounded more inspirational than Wayne.

Wayne takes three medications, and he still has seizures, though few people realize it. When his periods of stress are more frequenthe has more seizures. He had three in one day on the occasion of his mother's entry into intensive care because of flu complications. The only real problem these episodes cause Wayne is that he is not allowed to do some jobs that he feels he could otherwise adequately perform.

Wayne has lived independently for five years, maintaining his own apartment, and rides a three-wheeled bike, though he cannot drive a car. He has a "maid" come in three days a week, another rehab client living in the same apartment complex; he pays her $5.00 a week to clean, do laundry, and sometimes cook. When I asked how I could find her, he volunteered that she is more than a maid, that she is really his girl friend! Wayne joined a country church at age fourteen, but moved his membership to the urban church after coming to work.

Wayne maintains his own bank account, and though he says he has to live on a pretty tight budget, he is able to support himself. To cut his expenses, he tried sharing his apartment with different boys, but one drank heavily and the other smoked so he gave up the idea. He owns his own furniture, all paid for, and he is always neat, well-groomed, and happy. Wayne visits his ailing mother regularly. He said, "A person with a normal child just can't understand a handicapped person. It's been a rough, rough road."

Louise

Weighing eight pounds and three ounces, Louise was the first of three girls born to a dentist and his wife, following a "model" pregnancy with no problems. The doctor determined that it would be a breech birth, but she did turn and was delivered in the usual head-first position without forceps. After her birth in the morning, however, she had a seizure in the afternoon; the doctor guessed that she might have suffered a head injury due to a lack of protection in a rather late and rapid change of position, and he said that if she lived for three days, she might make it. Louise, whose head was large in proportion to her body, was placed on medication, but her seizures were never brought under complete control. She was a pretty baby, but although she was able to walk at fourteen months, all of her other developmental processes were delayed about six months. She appeared to limp slightly and to have lack of use of her arm on one side. Her seizures usually involved a sudden fall, and she never slept very long following one; they were more like petit mal than gran mal seizures.

Louise first attended the child development center at the state university located in her community. She played well with the other children, though she appeared to be sleepy much of the time. The only observed negative reaction to her on the part of the other children was that they didn't want her holding on to them going up and down steps, so the teachers tried to be available at those moments. At the center, Louise had the benefit of both a male nurse who was a Special Education major, who later earned his doctorate, and a student teacher who also received her doctorate in Special Education as well.

Unfortunately, Louise's physical condition went rapidly downhill. She was on two other seizure-control medications, and a hysterectomy was performed at puberty to avoid the inconvenience of menstrual cycles, an inconvenience that would surely have been magnified by her lack of understanding of her own bodily functions. A beloved daughter and sister, Louise died of uremic poisoning at age thirteen, with her family extremely grateful to the university and all those who had helped to make a meaningful place for her. Louise's mother always expressed her deep gratitude for the fact that there were always school placements for her daughter with understanding, loving, and caring teachers.

Rozanne

(This narrative was provided by Rozanne's mother)

Rozanne was born weighing 5 pounds, 6 ounces. She was a beautiful, blonde, blue-eyed, curly haired girl. Hers was a breech birth following precipitant labor, and there was difficulty in getting her to cry, but finally a high pitched squeal was heard. At the age of three days, she experienced convulsions from intracranial pressure; the doctor performed an intercranial tap, obtaining about 120cc. of dark fluid which he said was old blood caused by a brain concussion before or at birth. This procedure was repeated three times, with old blood obtained on each occasion. She remained in the hospital for three weeks with little strength and under oxygen for several days. She slept most of the time.

Rozanne was a very good baby, we thought; never fretting, she lay for hours watching her little hand as she raised and dangled it before her eyes, though her only crying was still high-pitched. Love, routine care, and feeding were all the care she required and she gained weight and grew more beautiful. At nine months, we decided to have her checked as she could not yet hold her head up nor attempt to stand on her feet. The doctor then told me that, due to her history, she might never walk nor talk, but that he could not say yet for sure. He advised seeing a brain specialist. The appointment was made; all of her reflexes were tested, and the report indicated slight mental retardation with slight scarring of the right side of the brain. On the way home I read the article, "The Child Who Never Grew," by Pearl S. Buck, which touched me very deeply. I cried all the way home and for days to follow.

At one year of age she was holding up her head, and before the age of two, she was walking and beginning to talk. She had her little normal baby flare-ups of colds, and she was checked by the pediatrician as needed. Sometimes he marveled at her progress.

At about age four, we began to be discouraged again, and took Rozanne to another pediatrician who adivised taking her to Vanderbilt University. There she was evaluated for ten days and we were given a similar report: that she will probably never read nor write, but might get some help from special education classes which were in 1954, just becoming organized throughout our state of Mississippi. Fortunately, there was a class in our town which she entered at around age 5. She attended only 30 minutes a day at first but was transported daily by myself and my husband despite our busy schedule of running a grocery store. Her older brother and one sister, both normal, went daily to school though sometimes they were neglected as Rozanne seemed to require all the attention. Then, one year later, she was able to ride the school bus into town to special education. I can still see her as she went down the hill every morning and came in every afternoon; she was the most eager of the three to go to school and come home to tell me of the happenings of the day. She colored, cut, and pasted, but books never appealed to her and she never learned to read a word. Her memory was exceptional; she never forgot anything, even when everyone else had. Sometimes I would get impatient with her many questions and tell her to go play. Instead she would go to the store and obtain more information from the customers, her favorite friends. They all took time out to have some words with her; I always thought they were trying to be nice for the family's sake.

Rozanne remained in special education, writing in her clumsy way from one to ten. This was her limit; she could never count nor write above ten; there was no reading of the alphabet. She could print "ROZANNE," from memory I suppose, as she did one to ten. She led an almost normal life otherwise from age 3 to 11.

She was always eager to go to church or to picture shows, to go sightseeing or on vacations. Fishing was her favorite sport, and she always caught the fish if any were to be caught. As she began to grow older she became disturbed because she could not compete in the things her older brother and sister were doing, we readily took her fishing or on a car ride to compensate for the things the other children were doing.

The sad day came when Rozanne began to become upset at the least little thing, going into temper tantrums which lasted for sometimes an hour or two, attempting to fight anyone or all the family. Often she told me, "Mama, I'll stick a knife right through your heart." At the beginning, we all learned to hide things in reach with which she might hurt herself or us or things that she would destroy—always the most cherished objects. Later, there was no remembrance of things she had done or said. At this point we realized that we would have to put her in an institution, something that we had always dreaded and refused to discuss. On a visit to our state institution where we filed application, we carried her through one of the better dormitories of small children. She looked around with very little interest, and as we came out and asked for her approval, she replied, "That's nothing but the nut house". +

We knew then that there should be no further discussion with Rozanne about this. The final day came; the notice was received indicating that there would be an opening for her on August 21, 1962. She was 12. This was the worst nightmare we ever experienced and telling her brother and sister that she would be leaving us was so hard. Convincing her that she was going away to school where there were other children like her, and that she could come home on visits, was difficult. Telling her that soon her brother and sister would be going away too—just like her—softened the news.

Rozanne was given a going-away party at our church by her Sunday School teacher and friends who had been so wonderful to her. They had never asked her to read part of the lesson, and she often asked me, "What if they ask me to read?" I assured her they would not. I was unable to attend the party because my heart was heavy with grief, and I knew that I would spoil the party. She received many gifts which pleased her, but the small things were her favorites. She loved attention. I used the money gifts for a piece of luggage because she would be coming home to visit, but upon arrival at the school, I was told I would have to take it home. They did not have room to store it. Broken-hearted, I took it back home.

We were permitted to visit her, finding her fine and content, and her housemother said she cried only one day, on receiving a letter from home. She was told that if she cried we could not write her, and she never cried again. Our visits were always short as she soon became tired; she seemed more interested in the packages we brought and what was in them than she was in the family.

For about five years Rozanne did well. After two years she was dropped from the special education program at the school because they felt she had advanced as far as she could and that someone else might benefit more from it. Never a Christmas did she miss being home, even if it was a day or two early, and she always spent a summer vacation at home. One week we took her fishing everyday.

The last two years her physical condition seemed to fail, as did her mental condition, which was finally brought under control with tranquilizers. She lost all alertness, her questions were fewer as the drugs took affect, and she could feel no pain. On a beautiful fall Sunday afternoon, I received a call from the doctor at the school telling me she was critically ill and being sent to a nearby hospital. When we arrived, I saw that her condition was grave. There was no hope when, six hours later, she was wheeled into the operating room for a laparotomy. A ruptured appendix and peritonitis had taken over and she never came out of surgery.

After the 80-mile journey back home, funeral services were arranged, and the following day friends who had never forgotten her or her eagerness to share a normal life paid their final respects. I felt then that surely some of their lives had been touched by her short years on this earth, and that my son and daughter had shared a love that I know will never leave us, a love that many will never know or understand.

Rozanne's Mother

(Author's Note: She was a beautiful baby! I saw her when she was 9 months of age, still unable to sit up, with a "blank" look about her eyes, content to just lie on a pallet. The mother said at that time she held a 3 month old boy and realized the difference in the "feel" of the two babies. This was several years before I had taken any personal interest or coursework in Special Education. When the parents first told me of the doctor's diagnosis of cerebral palsy, I was surprised, because my idea of CP was only of the shaking, jerking, unable-to-speak athetoid type.

After studying, I learned that she had the ataxic type of cerebral palsy which most outwardly affected her balance. She had a lumbering walk, and was overweight except in infancy. I did a psychological evaluation of her, at age 8 or 9, using the Stanford-Binet, Form LM (1960 revison) with a derived IQ of 69. She appeared to be well into the educable mentally retarded range and her lack of progress in a school setting puzzled me. She was highly verbal, had an amazing memory, and she always spoke in complete sentences).

Joey

(His Mother's Story)

I have always felt that new-born babies were miracles. When I gave birth to my third son, he became the miracle of miracles to me.

Already being the mother of two typical boys, ages five and eight, I was excited over the possibility of having a dainty little girl. My first prenatal visit to the doctor to confirm my pregnancy jolted me back to reality. He reminded me that I had never had a normal pregnancy, and it looked as if this time would be no exception. A miscarriage at the beginning of my fourth month terminated my first pregnancy. My second one threatened to do likewise and was so difficult that my doctor ordered complete bed rest for a number of weeks.   The third time was no different; after a difficult beginning, I had to spend a very careful nine months.

I had no idea this pregnancy would be the worst one yet. On that first visit my doctor discovered an abnormal growth that required exploratory surgery at the beginning of my third month, and he found fibroid tumors in my uterus. He explained that I needed a complete hysterectomy, but since I was pregnant, he decided to just close me up and see if I could carry the baby until the middle of the eighth month.   He would then take the baby by section and afterwards do my hysterectomy.   Meanwhile, he explained that the surgery could very well cause me to abort; however, he thought that probably I would not miscarry if I could make it through the first week after surgery and continue to be careful.

Then the miracle began.   I made a remarkable recovery.   My other pregnancies would never have survived that surgery.   Things appeared to be going fine until the beginning of my sixth month when the membranes ruptured, a result of the tumors thriving on my pregnancy and growing so rapidly that they created too much pressure.   I was hospitalized for observation, and finally sent home for complete bed rest for twenty-two hours out of every twenty-four. Nine days later, I went into labor, and after thirteen hours I gave birth to my three-and-one-half pound miracle son.   My pediatrician was so dedicated that she was present at 1:12 a.m. that morning, and I'll always believe she saved his life by taking him as he was born and going right to work on him.   It was with appreciation and love that I named him after Doctor Dorothy Alyene Reese, using her last name as his middle name.

She later told me that it took her sometime to get him to breathe by using an Ambu Bag and connecting him to the respirator.   She also said that if he lived, which she did not think likely, there were strong possibilities of his being blind, deaf, mentally retarded, spastic, or a combination of several of these.   As I sat and listened to her, I could not believe how calm and peaceful I felt.   That was my baby she was talking about!   Yet, somehow, I felt sure my miracle son was a gift from God, and I just didn't feel that He intended to take him away that soon.   She gently reminded me that he would probably be retarded.   I told her that if he were, it would be God's will, and He would provide a way for me to care for him.

I will never forget seeing Joey for the first time. I thought that all of his three-and-one-half pounds must be bones! His stomach would sink completely into his backbone with each breath the respirator took for him, every rib he had was visible, and there was a tube in his nose and another in his mouth held in place by so much tape that you could tell nothing about his facial features. Another tube was in his navel, wire probes connecting him to a monitor were on each side of his chest, and warmer wires were connected to each thigh. As I stood and watched him, I realized how helpless I was. That was my baby behind those windows connected to all those machines, and there was nothing I could do to help him. I could only place him back in the hands of God. I had to pray constantly for the strength and courage to accept His will for my son, whatever it would be.

The night before I left the hospital, they let me scrub, put on a gown, and go into the nursery to see him. They even let me touch his fingers and toes. I was utterly amazed as I saw hands the size of my thumbs, fingers the size of shoe-string potatoes, feet only as long as two joints of my little finger, and toes like tiny kernels of corn. His ears were about the size of my thumbnail. I thought that only God could make a thing so tiny, yet so perfectly formed.

I came home to two anxious and curious little boys. I felt at a complete loss for words to explain the situation to them. Once again, I turned to God and asked Him to help me say enough to satisfy them yet not enough to worry them. Once again He answered my prayers. They were patient and understanding—at least more so than I could have been in their place. After all, imagine being told you have a baby brother, yet not seeing him or even a picture of him until he is nearly two months old. I finally came up with the idea of taking a picture with a Polariod camera for them, and they were so proud and had to take the picture to school for show and tell.

Everyday for nearly two months, I went to the hospital and watched my baby through glass windows. I would whisper a prayer of thanks for each additional day he lived, thinking at the same time that the longer he lived, the harder it would be to give him up. I watched as they removed him from the respirator after twenty-two days and placed him in an isolette. Then I watched the nurses teach him to suck a bottle rather than being tube-fed; that took a lot of time and patience, and was considered quite a victory when he finally mastered it. I was thrilled beyond words the day I went out and found him in a regular bassinet like all the other well babies. I had to share that with someone, so I ran and picked up my mother, and we hurried back so she could see the progress he had made. They had carried him to be circumcised by the time we got back. We waited and got a good peek at him as they wheeled him down the hall, right beside us, back to the nursery. It looked as if he were screaming his head off, but not a sound was coming out. This was the first time I suspected that there was a problem. Several days later the doctor confirmed my suspicions when she told me she was afraid he did have some damage to his vocal cords. Thinking that only his speech would by affected, I passed if off as a minor problem. I had no idea what I was soon to learn about vocal chords and their functions.

Finally, after six weeks, I was allowed to hold my baby for the first time. They let me feed him when I could be there at feeding time. The memories of those times will always be precious to me. I soon learned, however, that I would not be allowed in the nursery since I had to have surgery, so arrangements were made for my husband and mother to take turns with the feedings when they were available.

One week later I came home, bringing my miracle son with me. With the exceptions of taking longer to feed and the crowing sounds his breathing made, he was just like any other new baby. I soon adjusted to his breathing sounds and, with my mother's help, managed to take care of him.

I had noticed the crowing sound while he was still in the nursery. They told me his throat was sore and that he was hoarse from the breathing tube. I thought that when it healed he would stop making the noise. At age six months, he was hospitalized with the croup, and a team of Ear, Nose and Throat specialists was called in to examine his vocal chords. They carried him into the operating room, put him to sleep, used a Bronchoscope, and found his problem; he had a congenital larynx web, which is scar tissue growing on the opening of his vocal chords caused by the respirator tube. They explained that the vocal chords close for you to talk and open for you to breathe. They found that the scar tissue was preventing his larynx from opening enough for him to get sufficient oxygen. It had not shown up before because he was so small and inactive but, as he grew and became more active, it would get worse; eventually, the problem would have to be corrected, and they described several solutions, though they told me that he was too small for any of them at that time. They also told me that his problem was a very rare and unusual one and that they were going to have to consult with other doctors as to what the correct solution should be. In the meantime, they planned to keep a very close check on him, stressing the dangers of his developing a bad cold or sore throat. The least amount of swelling could completely block his airway, and he would suffocate before I could get help.

I brought him home once again, determined to watch him closer than ever before. Everything was fine for a couple of weeks, but then he began to turn blue and have trouble getting his breath when he would try to cry. The doctors put him back in the hospital and clipped the scar tissue. After complications developed, he was moved to the Intensive Care Unit. Six days later, the doctors had to perform a tracheotomy, and his breathing was so shallow afterwards that once again the respirator had to take over for him. They were able to take him off of it the next day. He remained in ICU two weeks while my mother and I kept a twenty-four hour vigil in the waiting room; then they moved him to a room on Pediatrics where they taught me to care for him before I brought him home.

Once again my mother became my right-hand, practically moving in to help me. Today she continues to be a big help in caring for him as well as getting other things done; in addition, she is a constant source of moral support for me. For months, one or both or us stayed right there in the room with him since it was necessary that he be watched constantly.

So far, I have managed to survive many terrifying experiences. Nearly a dozen times I have watched him struggle as if his next breath would be his last, yet he continues to beat the odds and amazes us all as he pulls through with a smile. The doctors told me that a baby's chance of living with a trache are only one out or four. They explained all the dangers to me but said that with Joey they had no choice, and they have repeatedly stressed the seriousness of his condition and advised that I take one day at a time with him. They reminded me that his condition is quite an unusual one, but assured me that everything that can be done for him is being done.

He has since made five trips to the operating room. They dilate his larynx, which is only expected to give temporary relief; they will have to do this periodically until he is five or six years old. Then, the doctors plan to make an incision and try removing the scar tissue, which will, hopefully, be a permanent correction.

Today, he still has his trache, and he occasionally pulls it out. Fortunately, I have learned to replace it, and since he has to be watched so closely anyway, it has never stayed out long enough to cause any serious problems. He does keep me on my toes! Even at night as I try to sleep, I have to listen out for that struggling sound.

At age two years Joey is slow doing many things, but considering how much he has had to hinder him, he does remarkably well. He has been taking steps for several months now. His vocabulary consists of less than a dozen words, but that is only because it is difficult for him to make sounds with the trache. In all other ways, he is just like any other two-year-old.

In spite of all his problems, he continues to be a good baby. He has a sunny disposition and is very affectionate. I notice, accept, and cling to each new accomplishment as if it were the greatest one yet. As I watch him play now, it is with an appreciation most mothers know nothing about. I am sure of that because I have taken my own normal children's health for granted often enough.

Yes, being Joey's mother continues to be an experience, but a rewarding one. He has brought me so much closer to God than I have ever been in my life. The times he has been so close to death, I think he must have smiled because he saw glimpses of Heaven. As a Christian friend said, "That child has sent more people to their knees in prayer than anything that has happened in this town in a long time." Yes, he continues to be the miracle of miracles to me.

Stanley

(In March, 1972, I attended a meeting sponsored jointly by Vocational Rehabilitation and Special Education; Stanley's mother spoke, and this copy of her speech was requested to use in working with future teachers of exceptional children).

I am the mother of 2 boys. The oldest is Stanley, born in 1967. He was 11 weeks premature and weighed 2 pounds and 6 ounces. After 6 weeks of praying, we brought him home with hopes for a happy, healthy life after such a small start, never suspecting that anything was wrong.

No one was prouder! At each checkup we were encouraged that Stanley was fine and, in time, would catch up in size. At the six-month checkup the doctor said he had arranged for an eye exam—not with our own doctor but with a doctor I didn't even know. This was routine for all prematures, he said. I suspected nothing as we went to have Stanley examined by the opthalmologist who, without warning, told me our son was blind. The shock was unbelievable. No words that I can say, no feeling that I could ever communicate to you, would ever let you know how I felt holding that tiny infant in my arms. You, who have worked with and for the blind for I don't care how many years, will never know the heartbreak of that moment! It's always sad, and you are always sorry until it's your own child and then the horror of it all is unbearable.

I told the doctor that we had no idea our child was blind. The opthalmologist told me our doctor already knew—for many months. Why he never told us is still unclear. I begged and pleaded for him to tell me who to call, what other doctor to see, where to go, but there was no one to call, no place to go. His advice was: learn to live with a blind child!

The next day, our family opthalmologist saw Stanley and put him in the hospital for an examination under anesthesia. He came to us with the same diagnosis—Retro-Lentil-Fibroplasia. He was horrified! "This doesn't happen any more!" What went wrong? He had not seen a case of RLF in 15 years.

We asked for other doctors but no one could help, and nothing could be done. So that we wouldn't chase rainbows, our doctors would send us to the top man, Dr. Algernon Reiss, at Columbia Presbyterian Hospital in New York. He was the last and final word. After he saw us I was supposed to let Stanley rot without guilt feelings. After the examination Dr. Reiss didn't really enjoy talking to us since Stanley was beyond help. We came home from New York with a 7-month-old baby and not a hope or prayer in the world.

The phone calls we made, the letters we wrote asking for advice—I'll never know how many there were! All I got in response were booklets and papers, no one to help. There was no one to talk my heart out to, and no one could tell me what to do.

As Stanley grew he knew if the lights were on or off; in fact, "light" was his first word! I noticed that he could see things that were in contrast like lines on a parking lot. When I told my doctor, he said, "Impossible! No light could penetrate the tissue." I said, "That's not true, doctor. I'll never give up on him (mothers never do). Stanley is a very bright child and I live with him 24 hours a day. I know what he can and cannot do." No one would give any encouragement in any direction, however.

Meanwhile, I began searching for ways of keeping Stanley busy. He had a habit of turning in a circle and spending hours lying on his face on the floor. How could I fill all these dark days, dark hours, dark minutes? When night came, I asked myself how we could live through the next day! What would make him smile? I wrote to the American Federation for the Blind, and I tried to talk to other mothers who had blind children. There were some, but their children were older, so I still had no one to talk with, and with whom to discuss my problems and fears. There was no one to guide us! Why, why is there such a stigma on blindness? Why are our needs pushed to the back? Why isn't there a place to turn to in a large city like ours? We had problems we couldn't cope with and no one to teach us how to teach our baby.

We saw almost every opthalmologist in the city and talked to doctors and educators all over the world. All we got out of it were pamphlets! We stayed pretty much to ourselves in those two and one-half years. I became tired of people staring and whispering.

When Stanley was two and a half years old a friend suggested that we join a play group, and that was when we finally came out of hiding. I dreaded those Wednesdays because then, more than ever, I could see how different my son was; but we went, and I guess it was helpful to Stanley.

When Stanley was three and one-half years old we took him to see Dr. Arnal Patz of Johns Hopkins in Baltimore, the man who found that RLF is caused by too much oxygen in the incubator. Having given up his private practice, he is now just doing research and hopes to find help for victims of RLF through the use of the laser beam. He told me that most RLF victims are very bright children and that Stanley seemed to be as bright as any he had seen. We came home encouraged in one way; at least he had been nice to us, and at least he had talked to us and was interested!

Through Stanley's nursery school teacher I got the name of a girl who had taught visually handicapped children. At the time she was a 4th grade teacher; she began to tutor Stanley twice a week during the summer, and what he learned in that hour session was more than I could teach him in a year. He learned to ride a bicycle and ride well, even though we had the bicycle for one year, and I couldn't even get him to sit down on it! He knew the difference in shapes and could tell the color of each and which was bigger, smaller and medium. He learned the numbers by sight up to ten. That is what a person who knew what she was doing could do with a child on whom everyone else had given up. She represented the only help we had ever been able to get for our son.

In January, 1971, we were accepted to be tested at a center specializing in learning disabilities. In October of 1971, 10 months later, we were called in for a staffing, and we hoped that this might be a place where our son could be taught how to reach his potential. Maybe he could find an interest in something that he hadn't tried; maybe someone here would help him with coordination, teach him to eat by himself, anything! We went to that staffing with high hopes, but were told that Stanley was not retarded and, therefore, the center had nothing to offer him. However, they told me I could be helped by a psychologist and they were able to get one to see me on a weekly basis, and we are seen for home visits twice a month by a nurse.

Last summer we saw Dr. Heibert Solomon, an optometrist in Chicago. We were interested in seeing the new lenses he was working with and seeing if they could help Stanley at all. If any of you haven't seen these lenses, they are remarkable, very powerful, with not too much distortion. Anyway, Dr. Solomon felt Stanley was too young to examine at that time.

Stanley has gone back to school at the Jewish Community Center this year. He seems to be doing nicely; he's the last one in line, but he is in line, and for this we are very grateful. The coach works with him twice a week on coordination, teaching him to bounce a ball and to perform other exercises, and says he is improving. Needless to say, we are thankful to the JCC. They didn't turn their back on us like so many others.

So here we are in 1972, an age of medical miracles, and we can't even find someone to teach a five-year-old blind boy to walk straight. We can't help him use his knife and fork correctly. We can't guide him to use the little bit of vision he has to its best advantage. Stanley wants to be independent, and I want him to be, but he can't do it without help. And there is no help. There is no one in this city to tell us how to train, teach, play, or motivate, and we are decaying. Days go by with Stanley lying on the floor with his hand on his eye. This is a pity, a shame, a tragedy; a beautiful five-year-old doomed not only to darkness but also to insecurity. Here is a child who will not only never be on a team; he will never even get to watch the game, and no one cares.

Let's look and see what's been done in these last five years. Time marches on and, with time, comes changes, advances, new methods, and new ideas. So what answers will you give to the mother who begs in 1972 for help for her child? She will get the same answers you gave me five years ago—NONE! In five years not one step has been taken, and that's unbelievable. Why are these kids such a lost cause? In a medical center the size of this one, in a large city, it's a shame. Where do we go for help? To whom do we turn?

Please help me help my son to be a proud human being, despite this curse. Help him to find a place in this world. Don't chain him to the title of second class citizen because you just didn't get around to him. We will go anywhere and do anything to get insight into helping him stand tall and proud. Don't pass him up, because he's to him. We will go anywhere and do anything to get insight into helping him stand tall and proud. Don't pass him up, because he's too smart and too cute! Don't turn us away at the door; we have knocked so often and no one is ever home.

(Because Stanley's mother graciously acceded to my request to use her speech with various professional groups, the following letter resulted):

Dear Stanley:

None of us has ever met you, but we feel we should know you because your mother has "shared" you with us. We wish you could come some day this spring and let us meet you. Maybe you would like to go swimming with our other boys and girls in a university pool. Could you come some Wednesday, 12-1:00? We will be back in touch with you, if your mother writes that you might like to come. We are a group of people who will be working with children and, who knows?—one of us might be your teacher someday! We feel sure that you will go right on into a first grade, and have a resource teacher to assist you with Braille or anything else that may help you. And how nice it would be someday to have you as a student in the Special Education Department of the University—maybe even teaching youngsters who don't walk, or hear, or see too well! There is no finer job in all the world! We are sorry we couldn't find a red elephant balloon but hope you will like this one.

SPE 96 Methods Class
March 10, 1973

This letter from the mother came thirteen years after the first meeting:

Dear Daisy,

How exciting it is to hear about your new project. Your book sounds like just the thing that we all needed years ago. I will bring you up to date on Stanley's progress. Next month, March 19, 1985, Stanley will be eighteen years old. I find that so hard to believe. How can eighteen years have passed so quickly when we were trying so hard to fill them up minute by minute?

Let me begin by saying that without his teacher we could never have gotton this far. She is the most wonderful human being, the best friend, the smartest teacher, and the most caring person I have ever known. We owe her everything; she has truly helped Stanley to get where he is today. He is graduating from high school, #79 out of 251 students in his class, and he was named Youth of the Month by the Exchange Club of America. He has participated in clubs and groups of all kinds, but his favorite has been the Debate team. Stanley plays golf, snow skis, rode a bicycle, jogged and swims; I mix these tenses because Stanley no longer rides a bicycle or jogs. When he was young, he was able to do both those things, but the little vision he had was taken by cataracts and, though he has had surgery, he did not regain that sight. So you see, Daisy, somebody up there took it all, though he still has light perception. Stanley is the greatest student; he loves to study, and he enjoys the computer—equipped with a talking modum—very much.

The teacher began working with Stanley when he was in kindergarten, before he was to enter first grade. When he was six, he started first grade in a resource room. He again had a wonderful teacher and Stanley loved her. His original teacher taught there too; she was the Low Vision teacher. His teacher in the resource room was the teacher for Blind students, and both worked with Stanley. At one time he was using the Visual-Tek. Stanley went to the special school for two years and was happy there; it was a long drive for us, but we worked it out and were able to get him back and forth. Right before Stanley was to start third grade, a teacher called and said she wanted to talk to both of us.

She came over and told us that Stanley would go to a regular elementary school the next year, and Bart and I were both so shocked that we couldn't talk. It was five minutes from our house; however, they had no program at all for blind students. We were frantic, yet she wanted him moved, and that's what we did. She brailled all his work, and all the teachers were fabulous. Stanley was the only blind student there but he did fine. Then came the heart stopper—junior high! How was he going to manage moving from one class to another, having always been in one room for all subjects? Somehow, with the same teacher's help, he made it through junior high and then to high school, though by the time he entered high school he had to use a cane. I prayed I would not live to see him use one but I did. I could cry every time I see him walk with it, but we don't have any choice at all, and it does make him more independent. To see a young boy with a cane is killing me, so I try not to see him with it. That may sound terrible, but we are trying to be truthful, aren't we?

Socially, Stanley had only two good friends; still, he felt good about school. He did not feel "left out", although indeed he was. He spent a lot of time with his dad and me, but he never complained, and he never asked, "Why me"? He always said he was fine. One day he said, "I don't mind being blind. This way I'm special; otherwise, I'd just be like the rest of the kids." I said, "Stanley, that's what I prayed for each day, for you to be like the rest of the kids". Daisy, he has the most wonderful attitude. He didn't get it from me, that's for sure.

I must mention that he did have several dates during these high school years for parties that the fraternity had. I never wanted him to ask a date because I didn't want him to be refused—of course, I didn't tell him that—but he did ask, and they went, and he seemed to have fun. Once, a girl asked him to a dance. I want him to have a normal life, but I know that won't happen. I'd like for him to have a meaningful relationship with a girl, because I think he needs it to mature.

As far as books go, some were not available. Stanley was a great math student but couldn't go into calculus because we couldn't get a book. I can't tell you how great the school has been to all of us. Teachers, counselors, and the board of education have been more helpful, more understanding and more caring than I would have ever thought possible. We have been lucky in that area.

After 18 years, I am used to the fact that Stanley will always be this way. I really had hoped for many, many years that, with all the modern medical miracles, surely this handsome, smart, lovely boy would not always be blind, but I have truly given up hope. I never thought I would, but I have.

So where do we go from here? Stanley is graduating in May and has applied to five colleges. He has been accepted at one college reputed to have a very good program. We haven't heard from the others yet. I hope he makes the right choice. It will be so important for him, and I hope he can make it alone without his "support group" away from home. I truly have my doubts, but I know he'll try harder than anyone. I'll let you know.

Well, Daisy, I guess that wraps it up. All the tears didn't help at all. We have tried to do the best we could, but he has done the most for himself. I wish I could have been more help to him, but we had so little help from the "professionals" who supposedly know how to deal with the psychology of blindness and the "handicapped family."

Good luck on your project. I hope our story will be of use. If I can be of help, let me know.

Fondly,
Stanley's Mother

P.S. I left out something very important - the fact that we have had tremendous support from my parents, sister, and her family. My husband's parents were no longer living when Stanley was born. There was always someone else to help out, and Stanley felt a part of the family unit. He was always included.

Also, Stanley has spoken at several community meetings in connection with his debate team, so I feel that he has shown how visually impaired people can make a contribution to community life.

I have always said that my one wish is for Stanley to be happy. He assures me that he is, although I know he has missed so much. He was never a child; he was always old and always needed help. When you go to the dentist, people tell you to think of something pleasant, and I think of what it would be like if Stanley could see, if I could see him run or play ball or drive a car!

Also, I must tell you that Stanley has had the most wonderful father and that nobody could have or would have done what he has. Nothing was too difficult for him to do so that Stanley would have every opportunity to experience everything he possibly could—water and snow skiing, white water rafting, golf, trips, sporting events, and horseback riding. We have tried it all. Stanley never said, "I can't do it," or, "I don't want to." He's a really a good sport and such a good boy. I wanted to do better by him, but we could never get a break. Writing this has been good for me, Daisy. Thanks!

(Author's note: It is always good to get the perspective of someone who has a more objective interest in one of these children. The following letter, obviously, has been written "from the heart"):

Dear Daisy,

I'm writing to you at the invitation of Stanley's mother, because she explained that you had been in touch with her in regard to Stanley and asked if I would like to respond to your continued interest in her son. Believe me, I count it a pleasure to be able to share some of my thoughts about one of my favorite people.

My original contact with the family was at the meeting in 1972 when his mother spoke and I vividly remember her feelings. Two of us who work with the blind and visually impaired were on a panel which discussed public school programs of the visually handicapped. I can still recall her speech today—not so much the words, but the emotion. Shortly after this meeting, a professor with the Low Vision Clinic at a nearby university asked if I would go out to the J.C.C. to observe Stanley in his classroom. This was the beginning of a delightful relationship with Stanley and his family.

Stanley began coming to a special school while he was still in kindergarten at J.C.C. He met with us and began learning Braille. During the summer before he entered first grade, I began to work with Stanley, using some of Dr. Natalie Barraga's materials. Since he recognized his letters, we proceeded with some visual stimulation activities; he was eager and insatiable in his desire to see and do, and his attention span seemed endless.

In the fall, he was a student in the resource room, but I continued to work with him. He was able to use the Visual-Tek at close range. His print reading was slow, but his mind was quick. He wanted to know more, more, more about everything, and his questions were bright and relevant. He could get you started on a discussion of a million things—a teacher's delight. One thing led to another, and pretty soon I'd be reading to him out of the encyclopedia because I didn't know all the answers. For instance, blue whales were a fascination to him.

Knowing this side of Stanley and seeing him go to sleep in his classroom doing seatwork concerned me, and I became convinced that he should be in a more stimulating environment. When he was still in the second grade, I called the parents and asked if I could come by to talk with them; I wanted them to know that placement of Stanley in his own school system and neighborhood school was an option open to them. Since they had not known why I was coming to see them, I think they were somewhat shocked.

I went with the hope of seeing Stanley enter the regular fourth grade in the local school system over a year later; however, his dad asked if they could start him in the fall four months away, in the third grade. Needless to say, I was delighted! Even though I knew his Braille skills would suffer, I felt it was the right way to go. Too, I was aware that all students would be returning to their home school in the near future. Why not make the move before he had to go back at the junior high level, a hard time for any student? The transition was easy because of Stanley, some excellent teachers, and a great librarian.

Needless to say, the past 13 years have been taken one day at the time. I have done a lot of reflecting during these past weeks, due to the nearness of his high school graduation. He has grown up into a warm, caring young man who can carry on a conversation with anyone. To me, this is and always will be one of his greatest assets—the ability to get along with others. He also has a diligence and a patience not seen in a lot of students today. Working with him has been a unique experience which I will always remember. He's very special, a "son" to be proud of; it's not because of anything I've done either, but because he's Stanley.

Stanley walked those halls, went to class, carried the load, and found his place. He has competed with sighted students throughout his school days, and he has met their high standards with flying colors. Much of his school work has been completed with the help of taped books, parent readers, oral tests, late hours, and sheer determination. Never has he asked for a lighter load or wanted exceptions made, and he's never said, "I quit", or "I give up." He has been a constant source of pride and pleasure for his teachers. Stanley was the first blind student in our state to take the "High School Graduation Exam", passing with flying colors.

Yes, he and his parents have come a long way since that day in 1972, but not without a lot of trials and doubts. His mother still finds it hard to accept the verdict of darkness because she wanted more for her son. The pain and the fears for the future will be with them; they are with all parents. Nevertheless, they wanted him at home, and they've been there for him. The strong feeling of his mother and the gentleness of his father have all combined to make Stanley the fine young man he is. Daisy, you would be as proud of him as I am. Please excuse the length of this "epistle." I tend to go on and on about my favorite people.

Sincerely,

Ann

Stanley's story would not be complete without this final word. On May 30, 1985 it was my privilege and joy to attend Stanley's graduation and, later, to be the guest of his parents at dinner. He had won the highest debate award on Honor's Night earlier. He received the only standing ovation as his proud father walked across the stage with him to receive his diploma. Many family members were present, including the maid and nurse who had helped to love and care for him. A very attractive eleventh grade honor student—a girl friend—was there, also.

As I watched his mother dance with him, I knew she truly deserved that first dance! The entire family is going on a two week tour of England as Stanley's graduation gift. Then Stanley will move away to attend prelaw at a prestigious Eastern university. How I would love to have him as my lawyer!

His younger brother asked if he could be in my book. He may rest assured that he is, as he—with so many family members and friends—have helped to bring Stanley to where he is today. One of Stanley's graduation gifts seems so appropriate to characterize this young man. It was a simple key chain with the inscription, "I have seen yesterday, I love today, so I do not fear tomorrow."

Mike

(Narrative by Mike's mother)

Nothing was unusual about my pregnancy, except that Mike was twenty-one days late. The doctor didn't seem upset over that at all, but insisted, "Nature will take its course." Just after birth, an orthopedic doctor was called in to check Mike's feet, which resembled club feet, and they were put in casts up to his knees for approximately a month and a half; Mike—who was six weeks old at the time—wore corrective shoes after the casts were removed, and we were told that he would be okay.

Mike was under the care of two of the best pediatricians available, and though he did not crawl or sit alone on schedule, we were told not to worry. He did not walk until the age of two, but still we were told not to worry; however, a mother knows by instinct when there is something to be concerned about. I asked about his mental state at about this time, because he could not communicate, but the pediatricians said that there was no problem. When Mike was three, however, the doctor told us that there were signs of retardation and spasticity. We then took the child to other doctors who confirmed this diagnosis and said that an injury before or during birth could have been the cause; nothing could be done, we were told, except to give him the best of care and keep him healthy.

This was all extremely hard to accept, perhaps more so for me than for my husband. I contemplated suicide many times, for me and for Mike, but I knew that this was the wrong thing to be thinking. Only through God's help was I ever able to accept this terrible tragedy in the life of my baby.

Mike started to private kindergarten at age four. During the previous summer, the area trade school had offered speech therapy, and Mike attended these sessions and others for two additional summers before the program was discontinued. It was even more difficult to accept our problem with Mike when he turned six years old. I had him evaluated and was told that he could not attend public school. We did have a school for spastic children in the area; I started trying to get him enrolled, but I was told he would have to be approved by a crippled children's clinic in a large city near our home. A doctor examined and evaluated Mike and told us that our child should be put in a public school; he said that Mike should be treated like a normal child and that his problem was that he had been mothered too much. I had to fight the whole public school system, but they finally agreed to evaluate Mike again and they said they would give him a try in a regular classroom. I informed the local principal, and he told me to bring Mike by to be enrolled. School had already begun—a couple of weeks before—and I'll never forget the first grade teacher who gave me the third degree and refused to accept Mike. She stormed off to the office, the principal returned, and the whole experience was traumatic! I was crying; Mike was crying. That, in short, was the end of our involvement with public schools.

I learned about a school for the retarded that had been organized by a local woman whose leadership meant much to us. Parents of retarded children had remodeled an old colonial home in town, and twenty to thirty children were attending. Upon investigation, I found that the school did not accept children under eight years of age; however, by some miracle this fine woman agreed to take Mike early. One thing in Mike's favor was that he had attended kindergarten and was accustomed to being away from me.

I'm sure that she realized my despair, and I did a lot of volunteer work at the school. A few years later, our school became associated with the public system, which had started special classes for slow learners. This proved to be a mistake for our children because the teachers who had previously worked with them were replaced by the state with instuctors who had degrees but who seemed to lack compassion. The parents of the normal children didn't want them in the same school with our kids. Our children were upset and so were our parents. After about three years under this arrangement, we went back to our own system. We were sustained by various civic groups and by the United Givers Fund (The United Way); the Civitans adopted the retarded as their project and bought an old building which housed two classes for twenty-four students. We got our old teachers back then, as well.

In 1982, the Civitans leased some property from the city for 99 years and built a beautiful facility for our children. They received a grant, matched the funds, and the school was named to honor the founder, who died before the project was completed. It is now housed in a $140,000 building which has room for three classes. The school, which runs on the same schedule as the city school system, is still sustained by civic groups, The United Way, and by a monthly tuition from the students.

Mike is thirty years old now and will be able to go to school for as long as he wishes. The center is his life; he loves it and is miserable during the summer. Just in the last couple of years, the city has hired a therapeutic director to work with the handicapped and a music teacher to work with senior citizens and the handicapped. Both have done a great deal for our students.

Our children are trainable, if not educable, and it seems to me that no one back then in the field of education thought they needed to be trained. If it had not been for the vision of one lady and the help she solicited from civic groups, Mike, along with many others in surrounding areas, would have been forced to spend his life at home or to go away to an institution of some kind. Mike is a special blessing to my husband and me, and I have always trained him to fit into society.

I hope that you can use some of this in your book. I think that the biggest help to me was meeting other parents who faced the same problems as we did. It seemed to lighten the burden when you realized that you were not the only parents in the world with a retarded child and no place to educate him.

Shannon
(A Mother's Story)

Shannon was a special person with the most unquestioning and accepting nature of anyone I have ever known. She had a shy little smile that came easily even during the bad times, but I believe she had the spirit of a fighter. She fought long and hard against many problems over which none of us had any control, and she beat the odds time after time. I always think of her as my "Miracle Child" because she was a part of so many miracles. The first miracle, as I was to find out later, was that she survived her birth and the first day of her life. The doctors didn't think she would, but Shannon had other ideas.

Shannon was born during the early morning hours weighing only 5 pounds, 8 ounces, with spina bifida myelomeningocele. She was my first baby, and, as many young mothers do, I never thought there would be anything wrong. I had done everything I knew to do during the pregnancy to have a healthy baby; I exercised, ate good food, took vitamins, and got good prenatal care. I began feeling movement during the fourth month, which was just when the books said it would happen. Since I had never had a baby before, I had nothing with which to compare these movements; otherwise I might have realized they weren't as vigorous as most. I never felt the "rolling motion" that my mother felt while she was pregnant with me, but I figured that different babies moved in different ways and never thought anything about it.

I went into labor two weeks before the due date and had a fourteen-hour labor. That all seemed normal, too, for a first baby. I had been given medication to help me relax—that's how things were often done back then—and I was groggy when I was taken into the delivery room; still, I felt everything was normal. I even thought it was normal when two nurses—one on each side of me—began to press down on my abdomen so hard that I could hardly breathe. I had sore ribs for days and I found out later that they were doing this because my placenta had separated from my uterus too soon, a condition called abruptio placentae, which causes immediate oxygen deprivation to the baby and shock, pain, and bleeding in the mother. The nurses were pressing hard to help force the delivery so that Shannon wouldn't suffer damage due to lack of oxygen. The first time I realized something was wrong was when she didn't cry. I held my breath waiting to hear that first sound, but all I heard was the doctor giving some rather urgent-sounding orders to the nurses as the pace of the movement in the room quickened and reminded me of a film running too fast. Then she cried! She and I both breathed, and I felt that, whatever the problem, she would be all right now. The nurses carried her out of the room before I really got to see her. I fell asleep listening to her cries—strong cries—as she was carried down the hall.

When I awoke in my room, the pediatrician came in and told me about Shannon's condition. I'd never heard of spina bifida before, so I had a lot to learn. He explained that her spine had not formed correctly and that there was an opening on her lower back through which the flattened spinal cord protruded. He explained that there would be some paralysis in the legs and that she could develop hydrocephalus which would cause her head to grow too large because of the buildup of fluid and pressure around her brain. Maybe I didn't fully understand everything he was saying, but I tried to listen very hard and felt that if I knew it all then the worst would have been spoken, and I could deal with everything one step at a time. The first step was surgery to close the spinal opening, which could possibly restore some of the nerve functions to her legs, and at least take away such a direct route for infection to enter her spine and brain. She was very small, but the doctors felt if she continued to remain stable—now that she had survived the night—the surgery would be the best thing they could do for her at that time. The doctor also stressed to me that there was nothing that I could have done differently during my pregnancy to have made any change in Shannon's condition; and also, that nothing I had done had caused it to happen. He said that they didn't know the exact cause of spina bifida, but whatever went wrong did so at the moment of conception; after that, nothing would alter its course. He also stressed that having one child with spina bifida did not mean I would have other children with the same condition. Although the chances of having another child with spina bifida were greater now that I'd had Shannon, the doctor assured me the odds of having other perfectly normal children were still in my favor and this was certainly not an hereditary trait, even though it did seem there was a "tendency" toward spina bifida in some families. Shannon had a distant cousin, born only a month or so before Shannon, who also had spina bifida and who died from its complications before she was two years old.

These were some of the things that I thought about after the doctor left. This was also the one and only time I ever thought, "Why me?" Even as that question went through my mind, the answer was there, too. I felt God had chosen to give Shannon to me because He knew I could handle our special predicament. I didn't feel I had the confidence or the ability to handle the situation, but I knew that it was the only answer available. I decided to try to be up to the task, but I knew for certain that all I could do for Shannon at that point was to love her. I really didn't know where all this would lead in the future—what other problems would have to be faced—but I felt we could make it by taking one day at a time—especially with so much love and so many prayers being directed toward us from so many friends and family members.

I hadn't seen Shannon yet so they let me take a wheelchair ride down to the nursery. I didn't know how she would look— maybe sick, in pain—but I was wonderfully surprised to see a tiny, pink baby sleeping peacefully, with nothing except a square of gauze covering her lower back to indicate that anything was wrong. Later that day, the doctors decided to transfer her to a children's hospital for the surgery to close her back, and just before her trip the nurse brought her into my room. Even though I wasn't able to hold her, at least I could touch her and kiss her and tell her that I loved her.

The surgery to close her spine was performed, and the doctors considered the operation a success because they were able to close the skin completely over the opening. There were no complications, and she tolerated the surgery well. Where the spinal cord had flattened, the doctors had been able to cut out the knotted parts of some of the nerves and rejoin the ends. We wouldn't be able to tell how much sensation and mobility this would restore until later. If any had been restored, it would be a gradual process, happening as she grew and matured. After I was discharged from the hospital, her father and I visited her every day, even though we could only see her through the nursery window. We were able to see her taking formula and becoming more active and alert each day. Finally, we were able to bring Shannon home, exactly two weeks after her surgery. It was a special day for me to be able to bring Shannon home and hold her for the first time. It was just terrific!

When Shannon was born, she was not covered by any insurance. We had been in the military, and didn't know I was pregnant when we separated from the Air Force. We couldn't get civilian insurance to cover the pregnancy or birth since no policy would cover a pre-existing condition. This circumstance, which had the potential for being such a hardship, turned out to be somewhat of a blessing. Mainly because she wasn't covered by insurance and because of her birth defect, Shannon was able to qualify for aid from the State Crippled Children's Service (SCCS), which paid for all her treatment, including the first surgery on her spine, subsequent surgeries, doctors' examinations, diagnostic testing, physical therapy, and orthopedic appliances such as braces and walkers. The only thing we were asked to pay for, if we could, were her orthopedic shoes. At least once a month, the SCCS scheduled a spina bifida clinic. There, Shannon and so many other children with spina bifida could see all the necessary doctors—specialists in neurosurgery, urology, orthopedic surgery—plus the physical therapist, social workers, and the "brace man", all in the same place, on the same day. All these doctors had the highest reputations and were highly respected. Even though clinic days were long—a lot of sitting and waiting between seeing each doctor and little parking space—I was always glad to go, not only to see the doctors, but also to talk with the other children and parents and to share experiences. Spina bifida affected each child differently. There were basic things common to spina bifida, but the degree of involvement with such things as kidney function, mental capabilities, and hydrocephalus varied from one child to another. There was a common bond between the people at the clinic, and we were able to share the large and small triumphs of each child and to support each other during the setbacks that we all experienced.

After Shannon came home from her first surgery, our lives were, for the most part, as close to "normal" as lives can be in any household where there's a new baby. Some things were different. Until her back healed completely, we had to be careful in holding, bathing, and dressing her. My first experience with diapering a baby was different, too. Because disposable diapers were just being introduced to the marketplace, I used cloth diapers. When I folded and fastened the diaper with a pin on each side, the diaper would rub across the incision on her back, so I folded the diapers into a triangle and fastened them with one pin, the "old fashioned way," except that I put the pin in the back instead of over her tummy. This "backwards diaper" came down below the incision in her back and, since she always lay on her stomach, saved her the discomfort of lying on a pin. I decided that if I did have other children they would probably have to wear their diapers this way, too, since it was the only way I had diapered anyone.

Shannon's first year proceeded with the usual pediatric visits for check-ups and immunizations. During the SCCS clinic visits, the neurosurgeon's main concern was that she might develop hydrocephalus, so accurate measurements were taken at each visit. Most everything else about her first year was "baby business as usual"—first smile, first tooth, first words. She also learned how to roll over and sit up and how to get around the house by pulling herself along with her arms, which were becoming very strong. By this time, the doctors decided the paralysis of her legs was permanent. The hydrocephalus never developed, but during the neurosurgeon's examinations, he did find that the sutures (the "seams" in the skull which allow the skull to grow) on the left side of her skull had fused prematurely, preventing normal growth on that side. This condition not only affected her cosmetically, but could also have prevented the brain from developing normally; so, just after her first birthday, she underwent surgery to correct the problem. During the crainectomy, the neurosurgeon lined the affected suture with plastic to prevent it from fusing again. Again, we could only see her through a window, but she always greeted us with a big smile and entertained everyone by playing "peep-eye" with her surgical cap. She recovered so quickly and so well that we were able to bring her home in about a week. She didn't much like her "surgery" haircut—with no hair at all except for long, blond curls right on the back of her head.

During the next couple of years, Shannon had two orthopedic surgeries, one to lengthen her heel cords and one to release her hamstrings. After each of these surgeries, she was in long leg casts for about four weeks and took special delight in banging her casts together, much to my dismay. Also during this time, Shannon got her first long braces, and, for the first time, was able to stand upright. She also started going to SCCS for physical therapy once a week; there, we got instructions on how to exercise her legs to keep the muscles from tightening up and learned ways to help her become more secure in trying to stand and walk in her braces. We also got a lot of useful information on building parallel bars and a "standing table", which her grandfather was able to build for her to use at home. Shannon very much enjoyed walking in the parallel bars with her friends during the therapy sessions, and sometimes

~~they would race to see who could go the full length of the bars~~
quickest. Shannon also got a walker from SCCS, but she was never
very secure with it because she was afraid she would fall.

In 1971, I had a second baby, another girl, Michele. I wasn't
afraid of having another baby. I felt I had the information I needed,
and certainly I was aware of all the "possibilities." Even though
some people who talked to me expressed surprise and alarm that I
would even consider having another baby, it was my decision to do
so. I could hardly wait until I felt Michele moving, and when I felt
her "roll" and punch and kick in two directions at the same time, I
knew in my heart that she would be fine—and she was. Shannon
was very excited to have a little sister and loved to hold Michele.
When Michele started crawling, Shannon loved to crawl along with
her. I wondered if Michele's walking would cause Shannon to
question, for the first time, why she couldn't walk, too, but when the
time came, Shannon was almost as excited as we were. She never
asked, "Why can't I do that?" Michele became her "gopher" ("go fer
this, go fer that...") and considered it one of her duties to bring
things for Shannon from places Shannon couldn't reach. A special
closeness, a bond, grew between Shannon and Michele, with
Michele at times giving up running games with other friends to
spend time playing a quiet game with Shannon, or at other times
encouraging her to walk down the parallel bars just one more time.
Anytime anyone gave Michele a treat, maybe a lollipop or a cookie,
she'd always ask for one to take to her sister. The bond between
them continued to grow. As unquestioning and accepting as
Shannon was, that was just how inquisitive Michele was. She had to
know the whys and hows and the wherefores of everything. We
always tried to answer her questions as well as we could, which was
no easy task since each answer usually led to, at least, two more
questions.

In 1973, there were a lot of changes when the girls' father and I
were divorced. Shannon's spina bifida had no part in causing our
divorce, as it does sometimes with some families. I remarried, and
the girls and I made the big move to Texas to join my Air Force
husband. Shannon's medical care was now provided by the Air
Force. I had heard stories that the military medical facilities and
doctors weren't always the best, but the care she received was just as

excellent as she had received back home. During the next three years, Shannon again had to undergo several orthopedic surgeries to loosen heel cords, release hamstrings, and loosen the soft tissues in the back of the knees. She was able to continue weekly physical therapy at the hospital and progressed to learning to walk with crutches. These were very happy days for Shannon and the rest of us. One of the first things we did was to get Shannon a child-size wheelchair since she had outgrown the large stroller she had ridden in for so long. In Sunday School, she made lots of special friends who took turns pushing her wheelchair to class. Of special importance was the birth of a new baby brother, Brett, in late 1974. I'm not sure who was the most pleased—Shannon, Michele, or my husband and I. We never let Shannon's spina bifida prevent us from doing anything we needed or wanted to do; we went bowling and, with only a little help to get her to the foul line, she could roll the ball down the lane pretty well. She was in a swimming program carried out by a group of special education students at a university there. We took a family vacation to Carlsbad Caverns, and Shannon—carried in a pack on Daddy's back—enjoyed the trip through the cave.

Shannon was a bright little girl. She may have had a damaged body but not a damaged mind, and the time came for her to start to school. In Texas, there was an experimental prototype education program called PEECH (Program for the Early Education of Children with Handicaps). Shannon became a part of this program in the 1974-1975 school year, when she was five years old. Once a week her teacher, Rosemary, would spend the morning with Shannon at our home. With Michele being so curious and active, it wasn't long before it became a two-girl class. They both learned basic pre-school things: basic colors and shapes, the alphabet, the numbers one through ten, skills such as tying shoes, and how to obey two- and three-step commands. Rosemary also stressed the importance of Shannon's being able to do things for herself such as dressing, combing her hair, and helping around the house by emptying trash cans and putting away things in low drawers and cabinets. The intent of the program was to help prepare the child for school and also to help make the child more self-sufficient and a more "productive" member of the family. Shannon learned her

lessons ~~quickly, and when the time came for her to start~~
kindergarten she was well-prepared. We enrolled her in a regular,
civilian school, right off the air base. She loved going to
kindergarten, but was frustrated for the first month because the
time was so short that she didn't have time to do all the things she
wanted to do. When she was able to be in class all afternoon (12:45
- 3:25) she was very happy and excited to be learning with the other
children. She did very well in school; her teacher was always there
to offer encouragement, if needed, and her classmates looked
forward to taking their turn at wheeling her to the lunchroom.

Shannon never did things "according to the book," and she never
had many of the problems associated with spina bifida. She didn't
suffer any brain damage; she never developed hydrocephalus, nor
required a shunt; she never had seizures; although she couldn't
control bladder and bowel functions, she never had numerous
urinary tract infections; she never had problems with dislocated
hips or club feet. Just about the only thing that Shannon lacked was
the ability to walk. She was an extraordinarily "well" child and
didn't have a lot of the normal childhood illnesses that kids so often
have. Except for a few extra doctor visits and some kind of surgery,
usually orthopedic about once a year, she had a regular child's life.

In early 1976, all of this changed abruptly when Shannon
experienced a string of seemingly minor ailments. We noticed
blood on her pillow one morning that seemed to have come from
her ear. We carried her to the doctor and were told that she had a
burst eardrum, which we attributed to her swimming sessions, so we
stopped the swimming. She just didn't seem to feel well for several
days, so we carried her to the doctor again; this time, the diagnosis
was pneumonia, and the doctor prescribed antibiotics and sent us
home. Shortly after that, Shannon complained that her teeth hurt
when she tried to eat. Her gums were swollen, discolored, and
bleeding between her teeth; so on the morning of March 23rd we
carried her to the dentist, who referred us to the peridontist. The
peridontist couldn't find anything causing her symptoms and
referred us to the pediatrician; the pediatrician examined her and
went with us to the dermatologist; the dermatologist said that it
wasn't a skin problem, and after the pediatrician took blood
samples, Shannon went back to school, and we waited for the

results from the blood test. At 3:30 that afternoon, we had Shannon's tentative diagnosis: acute myelomoncytic leukemia (AMML). The rest of that day was a flurry of activity. Shannon was hospitalized immediately for a blood transfusion, arrangements were made for aeromedical evacuation to another medical center in Texas, and arrangements were made for the grandparents to fly out immediately to carry Michele and Brett back to Alabama because we would both be leaving with Shannon the next day. From that day on, the spina bifida was of relatively minor importance, and there was not a day that went by during the next year when we wouldn't have willingly given up everything we had to go back to the time when our medical concerns about Shannon were only about physical therapy sessions or outgrown braces or even upcoming orthopedic surgeries. All that those things took from our lives was time, and we thought we had so much time then. How quickly time had become the enemy! All of our energies, and her's, were used for fighting the leukemia. In one way, the spina bifida was a blessing, because during her fight she had to have a lot of intravenous infusions, blood work and chemotherapy that all involved a "stick" from a needle. Because of her paralysis, she had no feeling in her legs and feet, and the doctors, nurses and technicians made as many of the sticks as they could in her legs and feet, where she couldn't feel them. The pediatric hematologist even took blood marrow from the long bones in her legs, so again there was no pain for Shannon.

AMML is the type of leukemia that usually occurs in adults, so there's not much information on how to treat it in children. Her doctor started her out on the best chemotherapy that he knew of, but after a very short time, he knew it wasn't having any effect. On the day we arrived there he told me Shannon would probably either go into remission or would die within six weeks. Again, not going "according to the book," she did neither. She remained in the hospital constantly for four months while undergoing various protocols of chemotherapy in a search for the one that would cause a remission; however, the longest remission she had was only two weeks. Again, Shannon "rewrote the book", because she didn't lose her hair for a long time after starting chemotherapy; also, we had been told the chemotherapy would make her nauseated, but it hardly ever did. During these four months, my husband was able to get transferred to an air force base there. In July, we brought Shannon home and welcomed Brett and Michele back from Alabama, and our family was together again.

Shannon was in and out of the hospital a lot during the next eight months; in fact, except for that summer, she was in the hospital more than out. We enrolled her in first grade, and, even though she wasn't able to attend class often, her teacher and classmates were always sending her packets of "homework" and "get well" cards and pictures they had drawn. She got many cards and notes and flowers and surprise packages, not only from friends and family, but also from people we didn't even know who had heard of Shannon in one way or another. All of this was especially helpful for Shannon when her hospital stays began to get long, and we were forever trying to think of things to do to pass the time. There was a poem that stayed in my mind all the time during those days; part of it says, "Look to this day for it is life! For yesterday is but a dream, and tomorrow is only a vision, but today, well lived, makes every yesterday a dream of happiness and every tomorrow a vision of hope." We did indeed try to look to each day as a gift to be savored. We always tried to find some special memory to keep, whether it was one of the rare times she could go to school, or when she was home and we would watch the birds or the prairie dogs in the yard, or a day when she got a pretty card in the mail, or when we watched a storm brew from the hospital window that later was followed by a beautiful double rainbow, or even the day when her doctor "smuggled" two kittens up to her hospital room for a visit. Even when I would carry her to the clinic for a blood transfusion, we would make those days special, too, by stopping for a hamburger or an ice cream cone on the way home. There were always so many arrangements to be made, especially when she was in the hospital, since I would spend my days with her. Carrying Brett to the nursery, getting Michele to kindergarten and then to the nursery, getting them both home, and even just finding times to cook or wash clothes, all had to be planned. I always told myself that I just didn't have time to sit and cry for long, and I always knew that I'd have more than enough time to cry later. Knowing that tomorrow was never promised, each night as I tucked her in bed I kissed her and told her that I loved her as though it might be the last time.

As she had done all of her life, Shannon never questioned us about why she had to be in the hospital so much or why she had to take so many drugs now. Michele wanted to know it all, and we tried to answer all her questions as best we could. Brett was just too little to know that anything different was going on. With Shannon, I could only believe that, if she had any questions, she was somehow finding her own answers in her own way. I did question in my own mind why this was happening to Shannon, why a little girl who had fought so bravely and had already overcome more problems in her seven years than most of us do in a long lifetime should be faced now with such a difficult battle—one which she would almost certainly lose. I have never found an answer for that question, but I am not sure that even if I knew why, it would have made the thought of living without Shannon any less painful.

The doctors and nurses who attended Shannon at the hospital not only gave her excellent medical care, but also gave her, and us, a great deal of friendship. Once they found out that Shannon's favorite meal was spaghetti, any time she was able to be out on pass from the hospital for an evening we were always invited over to someone's house for a spaghetti dinner. We also became a part of the HOPE (Hematology/Oncology Parents' Endeavor) group, which consisted of the parents and family of the young oncology patients. We had monthly meetings and were able to greet new members and give whatever encouragement we could—talk and cry and even laugh together sometimes. We supported each other in whatever way was needed. Hearing first-hand the stories of the children who were getting better or who had gone into remission helped us all keep our own hopes alive.

Shannon had two seizures while she was at home on the night of April 1, 1977, and this time the trip to the hospital was made in an ambulance. She seemed to stabilize on the way and was able to talk again for the first time since the first seizure. The tentative diagnosis was that she had had a hemorrhage in some area of her brain. She was watched closely that night, but she remained fairly stable and was able to sleep some. As I sat beside her during that night, watching her breathe, I tried to find that same feeling I had always had before when she faced surgery or a crisis—that she would come through all right. But for the first time that feeling wasn't there. I prayed that maybe this could be another of those miracle times that she'd had before, but I also prayed that if this was the time for her to go to heaven that God would take her quickly. Shannon's body was never perfect, but her mind and her personality were perfect. I believed that the most cruel fate for her would have been to slip into a prolonged coma where she would be deprived of those things. Most of her favorite nurses came in for the morning shift. They all came by to check on her and say hello, and she gave each a little smile. Just before noon, while watching Saturday morning cartoons, Shannon died. She had another seizure and then just slipped away quietly, surrounded by so much love from everyone around her. Her last words—the same as mine to her—were, "I love you."

Her long struggle was over. We were able to donate her corneas—about the only part of her that had not been affected by the leukemia or the chemotherapy—with the hope that this part of her could live on and at least one person might be helped to see the world, maybe for the first time, literally through her eyes.

An autopsy was done on Shannon, and the final report stated that she had died of a massive cerebral hemorrhage. When we talked to her doctor about the autopsy results, we asked if he'd been able to learn anything from treating Shannon. He said he had not really learned anything new from her as far as the leukemia went, but that she had forced him to rethink his ideas about children with spina bifida. He admitted that he had always felt that a spina bifida child who survived would certainly not have a very high quality of life; but having known Shannon and having seen what a smart, happy, active child she was—capable of enjoying the highest qualities of life—he would always, in the future, measure the abilities of each child on a case-by-case basis. I think my mother put it best when she wrote, "Shannon taught us so many lessons, just being as she was, the main lesson being that we should take each day as it comes, be happy with it, and keep God in our hearts."

The only time I ever heard Shannon say anything about her not being able to walk was in the last month before her death. Her grandmother was holding her and telling her how big she was getting. Shannon looked up and said, "Pretty soon I'll be big enough to walk." If my childhood images of heaven are true—a beautiful place of happiness, where there is no sickness or pain, filled with angels wearing halos and wings—then I believe Shannon is one angel who turned her wings back in. Somewhere she's walking.

Don

(His own story)

(Author's note: During the summer of 1958, a course requirement of "Psychological Evaluation" was the administering of a large number of intelligence tests to people of all ages. All the neighbors, visitors to my home—anybody who agreed—were tested "free". There were only two of us in the class so we tested each other. Ladean and I know our respective strengths and weaknesses as no one else does. This gifted and talented fellow was one of those tested, and the results came as no surprise; though at times it seemed to me that no one, including him, would ever recognize his capabilities).

Almost thirty years! That's the period of time upon which I need to reflect. The past thirty years of my life? What a challenge this is going to be. There have been times during these years when I thought I was somehow the innocent victim of some rapid-fire changes that came upon me without cause or reason. I now am able to realize that most of these things occurred not merely for the sake of changes, but for the sake of advancement and progress in my life. They represented completion of a different set of tasks, or the accomplishment of a different set of goals, and all of that is not really so bad after all.

These changes started way back in 1957 when I left my home state to attend a faraway Baptist university. The decision to do so was more than just an adventure for me, although it was something of that as well for this country boy; it was a decision to attend a small Baptist school with a proven program in my chosen field of church music. I also needed to make that break—as painful as it may have been—with my family. Being the youngest in a family of eight, there were times when I felt I had six mothers and three fathers, instead of just the two very special parents God had provided for me, even though I was born when they were middle-aged.

The college years were difficult ones for me. My chosen degree was Music Education, but years as a high school piano student, a trombonist with the band, and a member of the glee clubs and church choirs had not given me a very solid foundation in music, especially in the areas of music theory and composition. Somehow, I was also not prepared for some of the liberal arts courses that went along with the educational part of my curriculum. I worked almost all of the time during those years— first in the men's dining hall. It was not a hard job, but it required my getting up at least an hour before breakfast time, walking the three blocks to the dining hall, at times in the bitter cold of early mornings, going to classes still smelling like whatever we'd cooked and served that morning, and being the last person to leave the dining hall at night. I was able to attend all of the university's special dinners, but while everyone else went with suit and tie and his favorite girl wearing a lovely corsage, I went with my white apron and work— uniform, for I was always either cooking, serving, or cleaning off the tables. It did help pay my tuition, however.

During these years, I became part of the drama department. A strong Christian theater director involved me in the campus productions of religious plays, and I grew to realize what a significant role this could play in the life of a church. I changed my degree program from music to speech and drama with a minor in music, even though it meant an additional year of studies. It also ultimately meant a mix-up in my transcript records which, combined with some poor choices and lack of follow-up on my part to be sure all requirements had been met, kept me from graduating with my class in 1962. My mother, by the way, was already on the first lap of her trip to attend my graduation when the news came, and she had to turn back.

I'd been offered a church-staff position with a suburban church in Nashville, Tennessee, and was assured that I could pick up that one lacking course at any of the universities in Nashville and transfer it back. I packed for Nashville, by way of Alabama and home. Leaving Alabama for Tennessee was almost as hard as leaving for college some years before. Daddy had died two years before, and it meant leaving Mama at home again, this time all alone. The work in Nashville was meaningful and good. I took a seven A.M. class at a university, and transferred the credit, only to be told that it was not a natural science I lacked, but a physical science. I decided the world would just have to accept me without a degree for a while. It did, and I didn't complete my undergraduate degree until almost ten years later.

At the end of my second year of working in Nashville with the music and youth programs of the church, I heard that the Fred Waring Show was coming to town and that any person interested in auditioning should attend the show and be on stage afterwards for an audition. I did so, and was accepted as one of the thirteen singers; I would be invited to join the tour just as soon as there was an opening in my voice part of second tenor. During the almost two years wait between acceptance and the call, I lived through one of the most trying and pivotal years of my young life.

The week after Christmas that year, I began having high fever and intense pain in my legs and hips, and I was diagnosed as having rheumatic fever. My thoughts ran something like this: "Why me God? And why now? Life seems just about to hit its peak for me. I finally have the chance to make a good living, travel, establish a professional reputation, become something other than a country boy from Alabama, and I have to be hospitalized; I can't walk, will have to be in a wheelchair for a long time, and the doctors can't even tell me if all of this is going to leave me with a heart murmur or muscular damage."

What a humiliation to have to borrow money to pay doctors' and hospital bills! What a child I felt like again, with no job, as Mama came to stay for long periods of time. How helpless it felt to be totally dependent on someone else for the simplest things in life. During all these months, I dreaded the arrival of the mail, for I knew that one day the letter from Fred Waring and his Pennsylvanians would come. What could I possibly tell them? What else could I do? I felt in one way that life had ceased to be important to me. Then came another significant change in my life, one involving a changed attitude.

For twelve years I had been in high school, for five more a college student, and I had spent two more working. In those twenty-three years, however, I'd not taken time to develop my own creative resources, and I decided that whatever else these months were to be, they would be useful. I read, I wrote, and I composed music, and re-established that needed relationship with God that, somehow, had grown dim and weak in the midst of all my activities and seemingly endless struggles. If there was to be a future for me, He'd have to help; I could not do it alone anymore. From that time, the changes I mentioned were significant. In the swiftly flying days that followed, I recovered from the rheumatic fever, and nine months later I was out of the wheelchair and on a whirlwind concert tour of one-nighters as one of Fred Waring's Pennsylvanians.

Later, I returned to school and completed my B.A. degree. I accepted the challenge of becoming the Associate Director of Church Music and Church Recreation Departments of a state Baptist Convention, where I was able to use all my experiences and leadership in the areas of music, youth, writing, arranging, drama, and performance. I began to see a less hazy focus to my life now, and I knew that someplace in the near future, the parallel tracks of my life would be coming to a point.

I was ordained to the ministry by my church. As a successful Christian single adult, I spoke, wrote, and performed for national conferences. As a church recreator and dramatist, I was asked to write for and direct regional gatherings, and as a musician, I was part of a group that sang demonstration songs. I was also asked to write the music for the first church musical for Senior Adults, or those over 55, and "Count On Us" has been performed hundreds of times since.

At a conference presentation of that musical, I learned of several possible opportunities for someone like me to go to other countries as a salaried volunteer with the Southern Baptist Foreign Mission Board. With a tremendous sense of excitement and a great deal of apprehension, I left the security of my stateside jobs for an assignment on the small West Indian Island of Antigua. My work there was to involve me with a growing mission church, teaching piano, church music, and working in a variety of ways. Nothing could have better prepared me for the joy of the work, and nothing would have more effectivly stimulated the personal growth I experienced in my walk with God, than His sunrise just off my cottage porch, which jutted out toward the open Caribbean Sea, as I awoke each morning.

Then there came another overseas assignment, this time to go to Guadalajara, Mexico, as a Director of activities at a new student center on the Guadalajara campus of the University of Mexico. My high school and college Spanish had been a long time before, but I found that after a short while I could actually communicate with the students. In my search for someone to play tennis, I met an unmarried missionary nurse who had lived and worked in Mexico for some years. In the strange and mysterious and wonderful working of God, our tennis matches extended to include time off the court, and in the summer of 1979, we married. It was a first for both of us. In the years since, I have pastored a church in South Texas, served on the Pastoral Care Staff at an Amarillo Hospital, and completed my Master of Divinity degree at Kansas City's Midwestern Seminary. In the fall of 1983, we were appointed as Career Missionaries by the Southern Baptist Foreign Mission Board and returned to Guadalajara, where Kay is a nurse again, and I serve as the Hospital Chaplain.

So there you have it, the almost thirty years from 1957 to 1985; years of changes, progressions, and directions. It's the story of a man: Who changed his major in college at the age of 20,

was a near college dropout at 25,

overcame a near crippling disease at 30

to become a professional entertainer,

completed his undergraduate degree at the age of 35,

married the woman of his dreams at 40,

and received his Master's degree, and Appointment to

Mission Service at 45.

I can't wait 'til I'm 50, because there is bound to be another of those tremendous life-changing experiences in store. What shall it be? The publication of my first book? My first major collection in Spanish? Or merely the completion of a wonderfully varied half-century full of life? Whatever it is, it will be great, for God is truly good.

Karen

Karen was born on September 30, 1959, following a long delivery of fifteen to sixteen hours. The mother was heavily sedated from medication given by drip, and she remembers little of the birth except that she would ask, each time she came to, "What's wrong?" "Nothing," she was told each time. It was a forceps delivery, leaving bad bruises on both sides of the baby's face. Karen didn't cry, mostly slept, and had difficulty drinking and keeping her formula down. She was born with club feet and an umbilical hernia.

At the six weeks checkup Karen's mother expressed concern to the doctor, who told her that she was just overly anxious and to forget it. By then Karen had become a very fussy, restless baby, and at about two months of age, she was found to have a hole in the upper chamber of her heart. She was evaluated and diagnosed as brain-damaged. She was taken to clinic after clinic, and she had speech therapy at a state university facility since she did not talk until age five or six. A hearing aid was fitted, but she did not adjust to it. Surgery was done to correct very small ear canals, and a cyst in one canal was removed.

Karen entered university summer programs at the primary level, and she was always well-dressed, pleasant, and enjoyed the activities and the other children. She learned to swim and was very fond of her teacher. She was thought to have slight cerebral palsy—though this was never verified—but she had understandable speech and learned to read. Karen attended five summer sessions, spending her winters in her school EMR class with a favorite instructor, Patricia Christy Granger, whom she met when Patricia was a student teacher. They had a good relationship, except that she did once bite her teacher, who bit her back!

At puberty Karen began to have petit mal seizures two to three times a week, episodes which were controlled somewhat by medication, and now she has been free of seizures for a year. Upon reaching high school age, she was placed in a regional education center—a public school facility for the retarded—and remained until the age eighteen, a period of six or seven years. Karen then transferred to a sheltered workshop where she gave the staff quite a bit of trouble, mainly because, her mother felt, she was bored. She stayed home until she enrolled at a mental health facility, aided by a social worker who had helped to make these arrangements. At about age twenty she was taken to a vocational rehabilitation office, where she was told that nothing could be done to help her due to her temper tantrums.

Karen reads Little Golden Books at about a first grade level, is good in arithmetic, and likes to color. She attends church and is quite happy in a Sunday School class of fifth and sixth graders with her aunt as a teacher. She keeps her room spotless at home, and even as a little girl, Karen would not allow her three sisters in her room. Two of her sisters are married; one is nineteen years old and still living at home. There are three grandchildren—a girl and a boy aged three, and a girl aged five. Karen loves them but is also very jealous and has to be watched closely when the children are around. As a form of discipline Karen is sent to her room. It is also an effective punishment to take away her telephone.

Karen's parents considered having a hysterectomy performed; however, she is past eighteen years of age, so the doctor said that it would be illegal for them to make that decision for her, and she is certainly incapable of making it for herself. There are about eighteen to twenty people who attend her day care center, and Karen—according to her mother—is the most capable one there. Her mother also feels that Karen, who is now working with typewriters at the center, could hold a job cleaning, washing windows, or even operating a computer. Karen has a good memory, at one time was an excellent speller, and has 20/20 vision though her eyes appear to be slightly crossed.

William Albert

On a beautiful day in June, 1985 William Albert sat in his wheelchair on a big colonial porch; a thirty-year old, born February 5, 1955. His bare feet were twisted. His cattle— farmer father sat in the swing to tell his son's story while his mother sat on an old church pew nearby, napping much of the time. The youngest of three children, William Albert was born at full term with no complications. Before he left the hospital, his parents noticed that his head fell backward unless supported, but the doctor said that he would be all right.

At times, William Albert's parents felt that he was more nervous than the first two children, and at age four months he had a bout with colitis which left him weak. In addition, his parents thought that his eyes did not focus well. He was taken to a pediatrician who did a reflex test and said that the child would never be normal. He was later seen by another doctor and given the same prognosis. A physician who came regularly from Mobile saw William Albert several times and prescribed a walker, but William Albert never learned to walk. An aunt suggested a faith healer, but the trip was made with no apparent results. At a cafe there, a waitress suggested that William Albert be taken to a hospital The parents followed her advice, only to be told to take the boy home and love him as he was. They shed tears during the long trip home, and again during my visit as memories of that day came flooding back.

At age twenty-two, William Albert was enrolled in school for the first time, at a facility housed in an old home and originally named in honor of a patron whose interest in the project derived from his marriage to a woman who had a retarded child. The name and location of the school changed when a community leader donated the proceeds of the sale of his late father's land to the center, where his brother was subsequently enrolled. In 1981, a sheltered workshop was built there, named in memory of a boy with convulsive disorder who drowned in a creek nearby. Thirty-two pupils are enrolled year round— attending each school day from 8:00 a.m. to 3:00 p.m.—at no cost to the parents, and there are five teachers. Each first Saturday in August a barbecue is held with all proceeds going to the center, and the P.T.A. meets monthly, except in the summer when it meets in alternate months. Contract jobs—picking up pecans, making wreaths, mowing grass, etc.—are done by those pupils who are able to do so, and a gift shop is maintained. The van equipped with a lift which is used to transport the students was bought for the center by William Albert's father. Until the fall of 1984, a regular van was used, with such organizations as the Lion's Club and the P.T.A. assisting in its maintenance.

At home, no pictures or door latches are placed within his reach. He makes wierd noises while attempting to talk, and has a very limited vocabulary, saying, "ma-ma," "da-da," "ca-ca," for the car in which he loves to ride, and "preacher," when Billy Graham—to whom he loves to listen—comes on television. Communication for William Albert consists largely of gestures, such as pointing to the sink, the freezer, or the refrigerator, when he wants water, ice cream, or milk. When his father's health failed, William Albert was forced to live in a nursing home, but his parents—both in their late 60's—kept him at home for as long as possible. They spoke highly of the center's director, and planned to keep William Albert enrolled there. William Albert loved school and laughed happily each day when the van arrived; in fact, the center meant everything to him and his parents.

At the time of my visit, his father proudly showed me progress reports which indicated growth in William Albert's self-help skills.

Joan

What joy Joan brought into my life, and into the lives of Dr. Jasper Harvey and countless others! A beautiful, well - dressed, outgoing girl, Joan is a paraplegic, and her story was related by tape at a very busy, trying time in her life, with her terminally ill mother staying at her home.

Born in Schnectady, New York, on May 23, 1937, Joan attended elementary school in Scotia, New York, and in the eighth grade, on Friday, October 13, 1950, she suffered an accidental gunshot wound that paralyzed her from the waist down. She was hospitalized for three months and from there entered the Institute of Physical Medicine and Rehabilitation in New York City, a philanthropic endeavor of Bernard Baruch, administered at that time by Dr. Howard Ruskin. For two years Joan had hospital teachers and tutors, but she was able to return to public school in 1955, and graduated with her class. Joan had to make many adjustments to life as a paraplegic, such as learning how to sit up, or how to get in and out of cars, and she had a real problem in facing people and admitting that she would always be in a wheelchair, especially at a time when not many people go out in public in one.

A loving family helped to carry Joan through many difficult adjustments. Her father never really came to grips with the reality of his daughter's life in a wheelchair, but her mother's attitude was to pick up the pieces and get on with life. Because Joan was only thirteen at the time of her accident, there were many traumatic experiences. She had a number of bladder infections, one of which lasted for six months. It was during college that she learned to deal honestly with her situation and realized that it was she who had to determine her destiny. She could go home and close the door on the world or be a part of it, and she chose the latter, learning to drive her specially adapted car, doing her own homework, and cooking.

After graduation, Joan entered a university to major in medical secretarial studies, following the advice of her dentist father and a doctor friend across the street who felt that they could give her good, sheltered employment, but after a year and a half, she decided that this was not for her. Joan and her younger sister, a nurse who was a major in the Air Force, looked at every college east of the Mississippi for a course in speech and hearing before Dean Healy from the University of Alabama called and offered her a scholarship, making her one of four handicapped people in a research project. She attended the University from September, 1959, to January, 1962, graduating with a B.S. in Speech Therapy. Joan married and returned to Schenectady, where she had already signed a contract to work as a speech therapist at Eastern Orthopedic Hospital. She worked primarily with physically disabled and neurologically impaired adults and children and served as a department chairman.

After a year in New York State, and the loss of their first son, Joan and Joe returned to the University to pursue their education. During her first summer there, she enrolled in Dr. Jasper Harvey's introductory course, where she found him to be the most compassionate person she had ever met and the most interesting speaker she had ever heard. After two months she mustered enough courage to talk to him and was enormously inspired by his philosophy that we are not here on earth just to get but also to give. Dr. Harvey, who was always very supportive of Joan, served on her oral committee and asked her the question "Can deaf people stutter?" Joan managed a decent answer, and when Dr. Harvey smiled at her, she knew that he was satisfied by her response. She finished her M.A. in 1964 with a concentration in the education of the deaf (Special Education and Speech), and—having taken thirty hours in coursework above the masters requirement in Speech Pathology and Special Education with an emphasis in diagnostic testing—was certified as a teacher of the deaf and hard-of-hearing.

Joan, while maintaining a happy family life—she and Joe have a nineteen-year-old son—has since pursued a very active and rewarding career as well. From 1965 to 1966, Joan was a teacher of the educable mentally retarded and demonstration teacher, a DSE, for a local city school system. It was during this period that she was responsible for setting up the first classroom in the city system at a demontration school for fifteen intermediate educable mentally retarded children, following classes begun by the University. From 1967 to 1970 in New Orleans, Joan served as an assistant professor of Speech at Xavier University of Louisiana; from 1970 to 1972 she was an assistant professor of Special Education at the Child Study Center of Old Dominion University in Norfolk, Virginia; and from 1972 to 1973 she was a teacher of the preschool deaf at the University of Alabama and for the Tuscaloosa County School System.

It was in 1974 that Joan completed her formal education, earning her Ed.D at the University of Alabama, with concentrations in Special Education, Administration, Deaf Education, Learning Disabilities, and Mental Retardation. In 1974, Joan became Director of Education for Partlow State School and Hospital, State Mental Health Department, where her duties included—in addition to certain administrative and fiscal management tasks— providing comprehensive educational programs, plus annual Educational Diagnostic Evaluations, for approximately 1250 severely and profoundly retarded students. In 1977 she became Program Director at Partlow, and her duties included the providing of non-unit based training programs for about 1100 moderate to profoundly retarded individuals.

In 1979 Joan was named Director of Region IV Community Services for State Mental Health, and assumed the responsibility for providing services to the mentally retarded in a twenty county area in southeastern Alabama. She was named in 1981 as Chief of Community Service Development and Applied Research for the Department, a position involving the administration, management, monitoring, and promotion of selected special projects in the area of mental retardation and other developmental disabilities. Since 1982 she has been the Director of Community Program Development, participating in an executive team management approach to the administration of services to the mentally retarded in the state.

Joan has also been a member of a number of professional organizations, including the American Speech and Hearing Association, the Alabama Speech and Hearing Association, the Council for Exceptional Children, the Alabama Association for Retarded Citizens, and the American Association on Mental Deficiency. She has dozens of special projects, professional activities, and awards to her credit as well. In 1973, for instance, Joan was named Handicapped Professional Woman of the Year by the President's Committee on Employment of the Handicapped, and she received a Faculty Recognition Award on Honors Day, 1974, at the University. In 1976 Joan participated as a panel member at the Conference on Professional Handicapped Women in the United States, and in 1979-1980 she was appointed by the Governor of Alabama to be a consumer participant with the State of Alabama Developmental Disabilities Planning Council—serving as Vice-Chairman of that body in 1981.

A treasured letter is the one she wrote me at the time of my retirement in 1976. She is one who really expected me to write a book!

Dear Daisy,

Some twelve years ago I had the pleasure of meeting you while working in the summer program at Verner School. As I recall, you and Dr. Harvey spent a lot of time trying to convince the City Board of Education that they should hire a new teacher, who was in a wheelchair, to teach the first EMR class at the university's demonstration school (other than those which the university had previously provided). This was a rather difficult task, but with your kind help and persuasion, the former principal of Verner School,

Mildred Grant, decided to "let me try" and my career as a teacher of the retarded was launched. I taught that first class with your help and guidance.

How well I remember those summer programs. It was so hot, and the second year I taught with you, I was three months pregnant with Chris and oh, so sick! You would meet me early, sometimes at 6 a.m., so that we could get set up for the day and not have to stay and work in the heat. That was the year I got to know you, Lila N. White, Myra Grady, and Reba Penn. Mr. Hitson affectionately called us "The Girls".

The years have somehow passed very quickly. They are full of happy memories of the many things you have done for me and for special education. You have always had more energy than anyone else I knew and still had time for everyone's problems. You have been very special in my training and teaching, and as a friend. As long as Joe and I were in Tuscaloosa, you have been there to encourage us and to listen to our various plans for the future. You were there the day I received my Ed.D., which made the day even more significant for me.

It is hard to believe that you are retiring. I know that you, George, and Ben will have a grand time with your travels and various projects. Many of us are counting on your writing that book you have always talked about, and I expect you to autograph my copy.

Joan

Chapter Two
THE GARDENERS

"If your believe in yourself and have dedication and pride, and never quit, you'll be a winner. The price of victory is high, but so are the rewards."

- Paul "Bear" Bryant

Never did that quote from one whom I admired so much apply anymore than it did to my feelings about teaching. As I grew up I do not really recall ever having but three ambitions—to be a wife, a mother, and a teacher. George, also had three options. He only knew of three real job opportunities for him: to be a miner, a preacher, or a teacher. He had seen his wonderful father leave for work at 4:00 a.m. most of his life and return late in the day so weary and covered with coal-dust and had listened to the hacking cough in the night from having breathed it all day, that he had no desire to follow in his footsteps. He felt that he was not good enough to be a preacher. That left teaching, so, after high school graduation one of his best friends, Clyde L. Jones, came by and said, "George, let's go to college." The boys talked until night, went home, washed their own clothes and left on the back of a log truck the next day. George may have talked to his parents previously about his future, but whatever family counseling followed was brief. The two boys left with a suitcase each for that faraway city, nestled among limestone level soil which was a sight to behold for these two boys who were in a new world away from the rolling, black, rocky hills of Walker County. Countless thousands of boys and girls came to know those two young men as "teacher". Incidentally, the couple they hitched a ride with had their coal stove with a sort of smokestack on the back of the truck and it drenched them with coal dust the entire 120-mile trip. Anyone seeing them arrive on campus would have sworn that intergration had arrived on Miss Julia Tutwiler's domain at Livingston State Teachers College at least 25 years prematurely.

My own teaching career was not so dramatically launched. My three goals were the direct result of role models in those three areas that could not be surpassed. During those depression years, being the oldest of eight living children and with nobody on either side of my family ever having gone to college, I suppose my parents could have discouraged me from the beginning when I talked of the desire to be a teacher. They didn't. On the night of my high school graduation, wearing a white organdy evening dress which I had made—renting caps and gowns was too expensive—Mr. and Mrs. Thomas Alvin Wootton, daddy's childless boss and his wife, put their arms around me as they told me again how proud they were of me and placed in my hands a blank checkbook to carry me through college and to pay back interest free as it was convenient. I always seemed to be surrounded by people who told me they were proud of me, expected a lot of me. I wonder how many children and young people grow up much of their young lives with no one telling them that—not because they don't mean to—but maybe just getting too busy. How many times I fail to do that! A small group of teachers saw me through high school with that same attitude, not just toward me but toward all of us (and I was saddened to learn two nights back that no other group of students will ever read those same library books that I read back in 1932 in a new three year old modern school because it was destroyed by fire.) When I think how that small group of teachers taught us every subject you would find in any modern school today (except for computer science) I am amazed because they taught us well. They were so interested in us and Mr. Ronald Wilson at our fiftieth anniversary this year said, "You are the oldest bunch of my chillun I've ever seen." He was our coach, science teacher, dramatics director—later became principal of the school for twenty-one years until his retirement. They were all just that versatile and taught for nothing when all schools in Alabama had to close because of lack of funds. They worked out a system to teach the remainder of the year just for us seniors in order that we might graduate. Of course we had to get there the best way we could. I can even remember that a group of us from

Coatopa sometimes walked the seven miles, but daddy usually managed to spare me the old Dodge to carpool my turn with our group. As I recall Vernon Rushing, Eloise Reed, and Bernice Husrt all took turns driving our group. Is it any wonder that I chose teaching as a profession?

It is a serious business, this teaching profession. It has many compensations, some of which are pointed out quite well by this theme written for an English assignment by a teenage girl.

The Advantages of Teaching

Since both my parents are now teachers, I have had a chance, firsthand, to see why teaching is so rewarding. In my opinion, the greatest advantage in being a teacher is that one is able to be with his family so much. I know of very few other students whose parents get home near the same time they do, who can spend the holidays with them, and who have the wonderful opportunity of "seeing the world" each summer.

Also, a teacher must be constantly growing. He must, more than members of any other profession, know what is going on in the world around him. I think this awareness and growth make possible a happier, fuller, more useful life. A teacher, by constant contact with his students, can never become completely bored with life and, therefore, he can never be completely boring to others.

A teacher has the chance to meet many fine people in his daily work. The other teachers, with their similar standards and interests, can become good friends for life.

Teaching has still another reward which few other jobs can boast of having. I see it nearly everyday as my parents look through the newspaper and read articles about their former students, as they receive letters from them, or as someone mentions their names. This is the advantage of knowing that, in some way, one has a part in a person's successes and joys. This is part of the reason that teachers keep on teaching when far more exciting and better-paying jobs are waiting for them.

- Shirley Styles

Before the term "Special Education" had been heard of, the following thoughts were expressed at a county-wide Teacher's Institute in 1955.

"At this season of the year, with Labor Day weekend just ahead, and the first day of school following on its heels, it seems fitting to look at the work of teachers and schools. So, let us together take stock of the work into which we are entering, some for the first time. One of the good things about teaching is that, not once but twice each year, we are faced with a New Year—with its inventory of past successes and failures and a renewal of resolutions to make the new one better. We have not only a New Year in January but one in September. If we ever lose entirely that feeling of excitement, enthusiasm, and honest doubt as to our ability to measure up to the task which lies ahead, we do need to take very careful inventory! Of course, we don't expect to maintain these to the degree which our new teachers will, but always our work for the new school year should carry with it these feelings.

"Many things have been said of the work of the world. Work can be a burden, a drudgery; but not our work! Not when we take stock of its purpose. To be able to do worthwhile work is one of the greatest privileges in life.

"Our work is a privilege and an opportunity when we remind ourselves of its far-reaching influences and potential. How great are our opportunities!

"Our task is far more than to teach subject-matter; reading, science, math, physical education, home economics, surely we need to do this well; but also included in our task should be careful consideration of the deeper things we teach many times without meaning to—those things which our children will need built into their lives for the times when it is not history or English they need at the moment.

"Let us strive to do well our task knowing that, of all the world's work, none is more worthy of being done with all our might so that we may leave marks, not scars nor blemishes, on the lives of those entrusted to our care this year."

- Daisy Styles

As special educators we have far more purpose than just meeting a child's basic physical needs. It is fine if the teacher and school can provide for these things: a good lunch and possibly even a good breakfast, fresh air and sunshine, a nap or rest period if needed, a restroom break every hour (or even every 15 minutes as has been necessary with some exceptional children), a chair of the right height, a green rather than black board, the elimination of glare from the windows, plenty of light, and maybe even much fine, expensive, specially-designed equipment to aid in working around physical abnormalities. These are important, but a memory for long-term events (even though the immediate memory span is getting weaker by the year!) brings to mind an occasion when a teacher, and an entire school staff, re- learned a valuable lesson. A real attempt was made to more adequately meet the physical needs of a teenage girl during the depression years, with the offer of a free lunch, some better clothes, and perhaps some pity all of which were met with a polite, "No, thank you!" Fortunately the teacher and school recognized their more important purposes, dropped the subject, and the teenage girl survived amazingly well.

We are not there just to meet emergencies; pity the misguided teacher who helps to instill in an exceptional child the attitude that his poor, handicapped life is just one big emergency. Thank goodness they are few and far between, and heaven help the intern, when grading time comes, who exhibits this attitude. She probably does not mean to do it, but the student gets the idea when the intern rushes to pick him up every time he stumbles, is overly cautious about his flushed face, calls his mother every time something the slightest bit unusual occurs, does things for him which he could do for himself, tells all the children how careful they must be not to bump into his crutches, and always lets him go first in line because of this, or lets him sit idly by and watch the others swim, square dance, or play ball when a way for him to participate could be improvised. She should not go "all out" with sympathy for the big girl who wets her pants when she gets excited but instead should calmly, routinely accept it as something which can happen to anybody, correct the situation as best she can, then forget it and help the girl to do the same. All life is not free from frustration, and the exceptional child needs to learn this early. Making mountains out of molehills, or even fairly high hills, is especially bad for him, for his teacher, for his parents. It takes a lot of discouragement and bad judgement to ruin a child; let's make sure his teacher and his school do not "provide" those things. There come to mind the words of a little cousin visiting his aunt. He said, when she wouldn't let him cut wood with the axe, "Aunt Mattie, there's just one thing wrong with you. You're just too afraid of danger!"

We are certainly not doing our job just whiling away a few hours until we can happily return our charges to their parents. We three (let's hope there are three people, but many times there may be only one) are the most important people in this person's life at the present time, and we should forever be a part of his life—and in a positive way! Sadly, there are forgotten teachers, or those who stand out negatively. Are the teachers you remember, for the most part, those who taught you the most algebra, or who read Shakespeare with the best expression? I had two teachers who did, but those were not the qualities which set them apart! They were also, and far more importantly, instructors who made you feel like "somebody," recognized what you could do, and tried to help you with what you couldn't do. Two others are remembered well: one stood a little, timid, dirty boy up in front of the whole class and "got to the bottom of his having stolen a child's lunch." It turned out he hadn't had any breakfast, among other things. The other one, also in front of a class, said to a student whose job had been to straighten book shelves and awaited a word of praise for a job well-done: "You stay in at play period, and fix the books right this time! The very idea of someone your age not knowing to stand books up rather than stacking them up on top of one another." Other pupils wanted to come to the child's rescue and say, "Don't you know there are homes without bookcases, with books kept stacked on the mantle?" But no one did because this would have just brought sarcasm for someone else.

Special education teachers are not missionaries! We have not generally felt a particular "call" to our tasks, and I don't think that we are above other teachers in this respect. Some of us stumbled into it quite by accident, others by a process of elimination because no one else wanted it, others by coercion (when a principal or superintendent really felt that we might have what it takes to teach exceptional children), others because of our experimentalist approach to teaching, others because of personal reasons (possibly because a family member's exceptionality aroused our interest in the field) or out of a desire for smaller groups with which to work, others because of ignorance (just plain not knowing what they were getting into), and it's entirely possible that one or two through the years have been attracted because of financial remuneration from the government for training in the field. In fact, we got some mighty good teachers that way! Let us hope, however, that none of these continued to be our reasons for staying. Like all jobs, ours must provide satisfying work, with a challenge, with stimulation to learn and grow as teachers, and opportunities for advancement. Amazingly few special education teachers leave the field, by the way.

We are not misfits and drop-outs from other teaching areas, nor are we people with no particular teaching speciality. Dr. Harvey often said that we must be able to approach any lesson in nine different ways. A good description of what the successful special education teacher must be was given by a student, Jerry Glen Pearson, when he said, "What I like about Mr. Styles is that he knows something about everything!" Heaven help the administrator who gets the mistaken idea that a failure at teaching in the "regular" classroom is a likely subject for his special class teaching position.

Neither are we "nuts"! Generally we know why and what we are doing when entering this field and will have the ability to make a logical career decision. We must allow ourselves ample time, though one year may not be long enough if we do not find work with exceptional children satisfying.

There still stands out the picture of a dear friend and former superivsor pleading with me who was wasting my valuable time auditing all those courses, not to go into special education where there would be no challenge!

We need not be retarded ourselves, nor crippled, nor blind, nor deaf in order to be able to understand and teach those groups. However, I will never forget one of the most striking teaching situations I ever observed. A blind teacher was teaching blind children of Orange Grove School, Chattanooga, and though there was also a sighted teacher in the classroom, it took careful scrutiny to differentiate between them. It is very encouraging to remember a statement from Dr. Harvey, that it is advantageous for the teacher to be as far above average, mentally as the pupil is below—a very good selling point when you talk to the Future Teachers Clubs—and all of us in mental retardation heartily agree.

We are no more likely candidates for mental or emotional breakdowns than the general run of the population; these things happen among barbers, carpenters, housewives, lawyers, doctors, and all occupations. However, it may be that administrators and colleges should look carefully at teacher candidates for the field of special education. Exceptional children and youth, and the demands of the task require a high degree of stability in their teachers.

Every word exchanged, every minute spent, every look passed between teacher and pupil is important. It seems that poor teachers, and especially poor special educators, generally fall into one of two categories: (1) those who feel "You have a lot of deficiencies, and it's my task to teach you everything you don't know and make you do everything you can't do now," or (2) those who say "You can't learn to do anything anyway so why bother?" How any teacher can walk away from her day's task and forget what it was all about or not weigh at least a little of what she did as to its value or harm is beyond explanation. This is not to say that she should not do some forgetting, and certainly the teacher's life away from the classroom needs diversion possibly more than any other occupation. My well-meaning friends said, as my retirement approached, "How will you ever be happy when special education has been your whole life for so long?" I hastily pointed out that teaching had never been my whole life, as much as I loved it! It is a serious occupational hazard to take one's pupils' problems home day in and day out.

There possibly is required sometimes a little more of whatever it is that causes one to accept the unexplainable, of dwelling on what is present rather than what is absent, of turning liabilites into assets as far as possible, and of helping students to make a satisfying life for themselves with only half the mental ability usually considered "normal", or only one-tenth the usual physical activity, with no vision or hearing, with emotional scars that would have long ago stopped many people from all usefulness to themselves or others, and with learning disabilities that make it hard to read or write. These are the tasks of the teacher of exceptional children which give meaning to the words of one professor, who said, "It may be that it is the teacher who is 'special' in special education."

So often I get the impression that a definition of education, in the minds of many, is to be able to expound in words that the "uneducated" cannot understand. To my way of thinking, it is just the opposite. I can recall now one of my most knowledgeable teachers, in a subject so foreign to me, who lectured in terms that even I could understand. This was Dr. Eric Rodgers, who even opened a second section of Household Physics for three home economics majors for whom it was required but who could not schedule it at the specified time with 150 students.

Just having served my first week of jury duty, I am reminded again of the serious consequences of experts not talking in terms which we ordinary people can understand. I choose doctors who don't try to add to my confusion but to lessen it. It happens in all walks of life. I recall a weather report from years back which said, "The probability of measurable precipitation is negligible," when "It is not likely to rain," would have said it much better.

Psychological Reports

The reading of psychological reports always intrigued me; for example, what do you really know after you read the following report:

"He has positive attitudes and emotions; his parents divorced, he has no mother. On the Machover test he scored on a 10 year level. He scored 4 on the L & M. On some of the reasoning articles he could tell similarities, but he could not discriminate differences. Also, on the Machover test he shows a rejection of the masculine body image, and he associates with girls but not with boys. He is not retarded even though he makes primitive reversal responses occasionally. As far as his mental development is concerned, he is normal. ~~He has a perceptual disturbance in the visual motor~~ coordination, and we need to administer perceptual tests for verification. On his responses to the Bender there were great overlappings of gap figures even though the figures and designs were not lost. He had a serious visual problem, double vision, prior to an operation and prescription for glasses. Now his eyes are focusing too much in the other direction, overlapping, or either his perceptual revisions have been more converging and there are misinterpretations or delusions being perceived. In addition, he can perceive general similarities on a 10 year level but he cannot distinguish differences, make discriminations, and reason, except on a low level."

The following report is a scream:

SPE 97/207

Name of Child: Odeipus Smith

Age: 8 1/2 years

Reason for Referral: Oedipus was referred by his teacher because of his disturbing influence in the classroom. He upsets the class by expressing rather strange ideas about his mother and father.

Family Background: Mr. and Mrs. Smith have been married nine years. Oedipus is the oldest of nine children in the family. Mr. Smith is unemployed at present and he is described as lacking initiative and ineffective in establishing interpersonal relationships. The mother is a worrisome person who appeared to this examiner to be tired. She seems to be a frigid woman. It is suspected that she has hypochrondriacal tendencies, as she has been in the hospital off and on ever since her marriage. She is not too cooperative with the school in that she never attends PTA.

Report of the Teacher: The present teacher is a substitute, but a report was sent in by the previous teacher, who lists her present address as the Bellview Hospital, New York City.

She reported that the child continually disturbed the class and seldom attended anything for more than a brief period of time. On one occasion, he worked very diligently on a special project of his own choosing. It was hoped that this might point up an area of interest, so he was given all the time he needed to complete this engrossing undertaking. However, it turned out to be a guillotine

Shannon

Joey

Karen

The author stands beside the school with (from left) Bill (the bearer of pears), Carl and Billy.

Rozanne

The 1969 meeting of the Alabama State Federation of the Council for Exceptional Children featured these major speakers honoring Alpha Brown on the occasion of her retirement (from left): James Hicks, Gale Lambright, Daisy Styles, Jasper Harvey, Faye Brown, William Center, and James Sartin./k/x

Alpha Brown is honored upon her retirement as Daisy Styles presents gift.

Louise

Billy

Wayne

Bart

Johnny
and his happy family

Don

Robert

Mrs. Mattie L. Madaris

These Livingston High School teachers inspired Daisy Styles in her goal of becoming a professional educator. They taught all the courses in grades 7 through 12. From the left are Mrs. James D. Browder, Miss Ettie Haynie, Mrs. C. R. Moon, R. L. Evans, Miss Lucy Lee Pruitt, Ronald Wilson, and Mrs. Thomas F. Seale.

Cottondale School
. . . where it all started

Wilson Dietrich

Tommy Russell
MR Program Chairman

Participating in the retirement reception for Daisy Styles were (l – r) Allene Russell, Lila Niles White, Hilde Schaer, Myra Grady, Virginia Joiner, Cam Pennington Saunders, and (seated) Joan Hannah.

William Albert

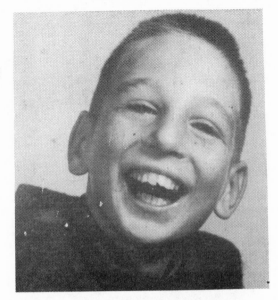

Dawana and her mother

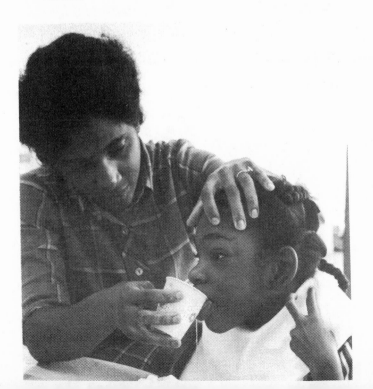

Daisy M. Styles

George H. Styles

with which he beheaded all of the white mice used in our animal study unit. Other episodes of annoying behavior include placing bamboo splinters in the teacher's spaghetti, and loosening the lug bolts on the wheels of a teacher's car. Thus far, only four children in the class have been maimed or injured. He seems to get along well with the children—as a matter of fact, only four children have ever reported him to the teacher. Report of Psychologist: Oedipus was a passive child who cooperated nicely during the testing situation. Test Results: Stanford-Binet Form L IQ 50; Form M IQ 125; WISC Performance Scale IQ 151; Authur Point Scale IQ 43. Discussion of Test Results: There seems to be a slight discrepancy in the test results on this child. However, the test session took 2 hours so he may have become fatigued. He showed no outstanding strengths or weaknesses on the tests.

Projective personality tests showed no evidence of pathological disturbance. On the Rorshach, his responses showed striking uniformity. He said every card looked like blood. This was quite creative because all of his responses were given while looking at the backs of the cards. Oedipus showed some hostility toward the examiner on the Blacky Pictures. He looked at the pictures and said: "These are ridiculous!" Summary: Oedipus is a quiet, submissive child who is functioning somewhere between the trainable and gifted ranges of intelligence. He has incorporated an overstrict super-ego which causes him to repress any expressions of his Id impulses. As might be expected with a child like this, he is subject to fluctuating mood tones manifested by severe euphoric-depression cycles. Quite likely this reflects a case of poor toilet training. More information is needed on whether he was breast or bottle fed.

Recommendations:

1. Oedipus feels insecure and rejected, so the teacher should give him warmth and acceptance.
2. Apply the techniques listed in Strauss and Lehtinen, Vol. I.
3. Be permissive.
4. Do not show harshness or irritation with him as this will increase his feeling of rejection.
5. Motivate him to learn.
6. Try Vol. II.

~~7. Get a thorough neurological examination—for the boy, not~~
the teacher.

8. Be permissive.
9. Have his vision checked.
10. Have his hearing checked.
11. Try to determine his interests.
12. Look for publication of Vol. III.
13. Refer to the Army Combat Manual.

The following is a treasured summary of what teaching is all about. It was written by two of our early principals.

Reflecting On Teaching

Teaching was always such a pure joy that I never really tried to put into words what it meant to me. I guess I should start by trying to define teaching; to me it means the art of awakening each child to his possibilities and providing the tools to help him become his best self. To accomplish this objective there are a few simple principles. I always believed in each child being important as I truly wanted the best for him and, in turn, wanted him to do his best. I was brought up on the old adage, "Anything worth doing is worth doing well". I believe the saying today is "striving for excellence". I also tried to enlist the help of the parents and to use the resources of the community.

Believing firmly, like Walt Whitman, that "A child is all that he sees, hears and feels", I tried to make my classroom as attractive and stimulating as possible, using the creative abilities of the pupils to provide a classroom climate where each pupil is not only very important but also responsible for working with a group and shouldering his share of responsibilities. I wanted them to experience the thrill of working together for a common goal.

My subject matter was important to me, and I tried to help my pupils see how the facts they were learning were related to everyday life, with the goal for helping them learn to think for themselves.

—Paul and Charlotte Jones

The concluding sections of this chapter tell of some outstanding teachers, bosses, and co-workers who made great impressions on me as I attempted to teach.

Eltie

"Don't go around saying the world owes you a living. It owes you nothing. It was here first."

—Mark Twain

Miss Eltie Haynie was born in Channing, Texas, near Amarillo, and was one of four children, there being two boys and two girls in the family. By the time she entered school, they were living in St. Louis, Missouri; they later moved to New York, where she finished eighth grade, and then on to Great Neck, Long Island, where Eltie graduated from high school. She attended Goucher College in Baltimore, Maryland, receiving an AB degree with an English major and Latin minor. Her masters degree came from the University of Alabama. Eltie's brother was president of the lumber company in Bellamy, Alabama over in Sumter County, which likely explains her going to York, Alabama to teach for three years. She also spent a year in Livingston, Alabama, before going to France for a year as a tutor for the children of an American family.

Upon her return from Europe, it was my happy privilege to enroll in her seventh grade class at Livingston High School. This was over fifty years ago, in the midst of the Great Depression. I can still picture the two dresses she wore alternately one year, and Miss Haynie recalls the school publication which carried an article entitled, "Miss Haynie Finally Able to Buy a New Blue Skirt." Her pay—when there was any—was forty dollars a month, and teachers went without pay a part of one school year (1936) so that the seniors could graduate.

Miss Haynie introduced me to good literature, including Dickens and other classics, and I can still see her holding us spellbound by reading Ivanhoe aloud. She had the special interest in her pupils which is so necessary for a teacher, and she is still the center of attention at our class reunion! We recently held our fiftieth, and we were saddened by Miss Haynie's absence. She proofed my manuscript from her wheelchair after a broken hip, and what a joy it was to visit her! Except for her influence, and that of other good teachers, I would never have made a career in education.

Jasper

"The world stands aside to let anyone pass who knows where he is going."

- Jordon

The world did indeed stand aside for Dr. Jasper E. Harvey, and it is almost as though I can still hear him saying, "Just call me Jasper, or Jas, old boy," as he often referred to himself. This was a difficult request with which to comply, especially when one had built up years of respect for the man, and even after I ceased to be his student and had become his co- worker, informal terms of address seemed inappropriate. It is hard to believe that Dr. Harvey is no longer with us. He passed away after a brief illness at the age of fifty-six, on November 27, 1980, in an Austin, Texas hospital, and was buried in Elmwood Memorial Park in Abilene.

Our paths first crossed in 1959, when George came home from a principals' meeting and said, "I heard a speaker today whom you would really enjoy!" How truthfully he spoke, because that speaker was Jasper Harvey. At the time I was making feeble attempts to teach the special class at Cottondale School, following on the heels of a delightful speech therapist who had taught the class for only the spring semester of the previous school year. There were thirty-nine first graders in my group, so it would be foolish for me to claim that I was actually "teaching" anyone anything. "Surely," I thought, "there must be groups smaller than this!"

Through my years of teaching, I often experienced regrets at the end of school years, speculating on what else might have been done for many students who tried very hard to learn, yet who needed more time and attention than I could give them. It was this sense of a job left partially done which prompted me to take more courses at the University, even though I had completed my M.A. in 1950 and was not seeking a further degree. One particularly interesting course which I audited, and eventually took for credit, was "The Exceptional School Child," with an absolutely fascinating textbook by Kirk and Johnson called *Educating the Retarded*. I can honestly say that I have never read another book with such interest.

I'll never forget the day that I went to speak to Dr. Harvey about my program of extra study, because never had there been a professor who was any more interested or any more willing to be of help. He told me that it would be acceptable to audit his courses, especially since I had two teenagers at home who needed more time with their mother than I could have spared if I had been writing papers and studying for tests. I sat in on Dr. Harvey's night course that spring semester, and spent a full summer term auditing every class he taught.

It was Dr. Harvey who warned me in advance of the certification requirements and standards of special education in Alabama to be initiated by Mrs. Alpha Brown. Mrs. Brown, from Arkansas, had been on the scene since 1956 as a consultant with the State Department of Education. It was Mrs. Brown who convinced Jasper to come to Alabama in 1959, and together they changed the face of special education in this state.

Anyone who didn't know Mrs. Brown certainly missed something! Can you imagine a lady whose mind could not be changed, and whose feeling toward "exceptionalities" was to make no exception? You didn't even try to change her mind, so when I became aware of the certification requirements, I proceeded to enroll for a number of courses which I had already audited, and was able to actually pass them. It was Dr. Lucille Sexton with whom I finally took "The Exceptional School Child" for credit, after having audited the course with Dr. Strunk and Dr. Harvey. I was never bored with the class because I had learned by then about individual differences and it was a joy to work with those four delightful individuals. Almost without intending it, I earned my AA certification.

By way of further biographical information, Dr. Harvey—born July 15, 1924, in Sweetwater, Texas—began teaching in the Texas City, Texas Independent School District in the area of the mentally retarded in September, 1952, after earning his B.A. in Zoology and his M.Ed.—with a major in Educational Psychology, Area of Exceptional Children—from the University of Texas at Austin. Jas, who was also an Army veteran, having served as a surgical nurse and instructor of medical technicians from 1944 to 1946, earned his

Ph.D. at Texas in 1960—with another major in Educational Psychology, and a minor in Speech Pathology and Audiology.

From 1959 to 1969, Jas was Chairman of the Department of Special Education at the University of Alabama, as well as consultant to the State Committee on the Education of Exceptional Children, and from 1969 to 1973, he was department chairman at the University of Texas. From 1976 until his death in 1980, Jas served as director of the Division of Personnel Preparation, Bureau of Education. He was listed in *Who's Who in America,* and in *Who's Who in the World.*

Because of Jas' stature in the field of special education, his untimely death certainly did not go unnoticed or unmourned. In February, 1981, in the bulletin of the Texas Federation Council for Exceptional Children, the president of that group stated, "Special educators everywhere, but especially in Texas, truly experienced a tremendous loss with the recent death of one of the most respected special educators," and mentioned Jasper's "wisdom and enthusiasm." In the February, 1981 issue of *Exceptional Children,* the publication of the Council for Exceptional Children, Dr. Harvey was remembered as "an outstanding special educator" who made "significant contributions to the profession."

Perhaps the most eloquent tribute to Jasper Harvey came from Dr. Judy Smith-Davis, writing in the newsletter *Counterpoint*—a publication sponsored by the National Association of State Directors of Special Education—in November, 1980. After briefly outlining Dr. Harvey's rich and varied thirty-year career, she offered the following remarks.

"Jasper was a man of remarkably high standards of quality and integrity and responsibility. His work was his pleasure. He demanded a great deal of himself, and he sought these standards in others and in their work. He wanted to make things better and he wanted us to make things better—not only in the context of teaching, not only in the conditions in which handicapped individuals live and learn, but also the quality of their lives and our work. His influence and his concern for quality touched many of us.

Jasper was also a man of great good humor and wit, which not many people understood— a fact that sometimes disappointed him. In this and other ways, he was, in a sense, alone. His particular dedication and the position he held often separated him from the rest of us. He was a proud man. He took great pride in his work and in his profession, and he was proud of his colleagues and what they were accomplishing. He was knowledgeable in detail about hundreds of projects and programs across the country, in a depth that might have astounded their staffs—and he followed their progress with interest and admiration and great hope. Many—indeed thousands—reciprocated that pride and admiration. During the past few months, Jasper received a constant and undiminished avalanche of letters and cards and visits and messages and calls and remembrances. He was genuinely touched and moved by this demonstration of affection, respect, and concern. It meant that his goals, what he had done and what he had tried to do, had been understood and valued.

Jasper is gone, but the rest of us are still here, endeavoring to create a better profession, a better system of education, a better society. In this endeavor, let us understand and value and support the best in one another. Let us be kind. Let us be concerned for one another, let us take pride and interest in one another's work, and let us communicate this to each other - not later, but sooner."

THE UNIVERSITY OF TEXAS AT AUSTIN
COLLEGE OF EDUCATION
AUSTIN, TEXAS 78712

Department of Special Education
Telephone: (512) 471-4161

February 2, 1976

Dear Daisy,

Congratulations on your retirement! One thing, though, you're entirely too young to do such a thing.

I talked with Tommy Russell last week while I was in Washington and he told me of the reception planned for you and the bound volume they will be putting together with letters from young and old who over the years have loved and appreciated you. It would be my pleasure to be with you on the 15th at the reception, but it just is not possible.

We lived through so many things together in the 1960's. It is difficult to put on paper the many indebtednesses I owe you, as well as my appreciation for knowledges and skills you shared with me with patience through the Alabama years.

I learned in Alabama the saying that a good teacher lives forever through the lives of those she touches. This you surely will do, for your span included many young and emerging individuals up through beginning college and university professors. You really discovered Hilde Schaer—and what a loss it would have been not seeing her to a terminal degree. Of course, she was one of many, but one we both shared tangentially.

Your contributions could be listed in volumes, but the unknown and unsung kinds of things wholly given by you to people have been the great ones.

Jasper

Wilson

Department Chairman 1969-72

I first knew Wilson L. Dietrich in a teacher-student relationship. Wilson attended Slippery Rock College, Pennsyvania, graduating in 1958 with a degree in Health Education, received a master's degree in School Administration in 1964, from Appalachian State University, Boone, North Carolina, and Ed.D. in Curriculum Study and Research with a concentration in Special Education in 1967, from the University of Alabama. His years of professional experience include five years as a teacher in various areas of Special Education in Ft. Lauderdale, Florida. At Appalachian State, Wilson served as critic-teacher in the laboratory school were he supervised student instructors, and served for two years in Tuscaloosa as coordinator of the Hackberry Project, our residential summer program for crippled children. More recently he has served as first Educational consultant, Center for Developmental and Learning Disorders, at the Medical College in Birmingham. He and Amy have two children. He writes:

Dear Daisy,

Thank you for sending me the material regarding the forthcoming book. Since the majority of the information about me really related more to when I was a student rather than chairman,

I've tried to think of some other information pertinent to my "boss" days. I don't know if it can be said in a book but the hardest chore I faced was to try and hold the department together after Jasper left. It was certainly unique to become Chairman less than 2 years after I graduated from the department. To say I was "wet behind the ears" is to put it mildly. Because of Jasper's strong personality and the success of receiving large amounts of federal and state grants, my task was hard. My earliest ally was, surprisingly, Ray Fowler of Psychology, so my development of a cross-campus relationship with that department ranks high in my memory of significant achievements. The development of the program for emotionally disturbed students on campus occurred during this time and Butch and Lew were instrumental in getting this going. I also spent many hours in helping the pre-vocational and vocational programs get off the ground at Partlow. That was particularly satisfying in view of court orders and the "new" emphasis in 1986 on transition. We were doing that, successfully, in 1970.

I was proud to serve as 1st Vice President of the Alabama CEC in 1969-70 and President in 1970-71. Also, in 1969-71, I served as Chairman, General Section, Southeastern AAMD (American Assocaition on Mental Deficiency).

During my tenure, the department received approval for an undergraduate degree in Special Education. I had Marion Thompson provide the leadership for that, and he did a superb job. Jack Stewart and I developed the first "Handbook for Organization and Administration of Local Special Education Programs" for the State Department.

After a conversation with Paul Orr, I began dialogue with vocational rehabilitation regarding the renovation of Graves Hall to meet the needs of the handicapped. From that beginning a University committee was formed, on which I served, that did a massive survey of the campus prior to the mandates of Section 504. The university should be very proud of those pioneering efforts. (I never have ridden the elevator in Graves Hall).

I guess that I did more than I remembered before I started this and I'm sure some things were left out. The two years (1969- 71) that I served as chairman were difficult, I did learn a lot in a hurry. I hope it assisted in my leadership abilities here at Memphis State.

For the past six years, I have been the chairman of state planning for the mentally retarded along with my duties as a professor.

Best Wishes,
Wilson

Bob

Dr. Bob Palk died of leukemia in October, 1985, and his passing represented a great loss to his family and friends, his fellow workers, and to Special Education in general. Bob came to the University of Alabama from the Bureau of Education for the Handicapped, Washington, D.C., in August, 1972. He taught general Special Education courses as well as those in the area of Mental Retardation, headed the undergraduate program, and was acting chairman of the department during the spring semester of 1975. Bob once related the following anecdotes.

"My beard caused some concern when I first came to the University. Beards were then not generally accepted by local school personnel. Once, when I was going into a school to supervise some students, a young pupil looked at me with wide eyes and asked, 'Is you Abraham Lincoln?' On another occasion," Bob continued, "a patient came up to me at Bryce Hospital, pointed to my beard, and laughed and laughed. He said, 'You swallowed a mule and left his tail hanging out.'" I even recall his telling of the values of a beard—he claimed that it enhanced certain manly characteristics—when I first heard him as a speaker in Montgomery. I went home feeling sorry for my husband George, who only grew a beard when he was in the army, 12,000 miles away in New Guinea. I learned, during an interim class on camping, when Bob invited my Arts and Crafts class over to learn macrame, that he held his loops of cords with his big toe. My students and I were unable ever to duplicate that!

After our trip to C.E.C. in Los Angeles, Bob swore never to travel on the same plane with me again. It was a night flight, and he was across the aisle trying to get some rest; my son Ben was curled up beside me, also asleep. I don't sleep much on planes—not even much when I'm at home in bed—so I always take along some handwork or reading matter. This particular time, I was into flower garden quilts. All the stewardesses, as well as passengers on the way to the restroom, would stop and ask me about my piecing. I disturbed all 320 passengers when I dropped my thimble and nearly everybody tried to help me find it. I've often wondered what the one or two people who remained in their seats trying to sleep, thought when a stewardess crawled by on her knees looking for a thimble.

Dr. Palk died of leukemia in October, 1985, having taught through the summer session ending in August. The only person who, early on, read and proofed my entire manuscript of *A Pear for the Teacher,* he made many helpful suggestions; in fact, the outline I have used is entirely at his recommendation, making use of his reference to growing children being similar to growing plants. I will never forget the kind comment he made when he returned the manuscript; "You really shot my week. Once I began reading, I could not put it down." What a friend Special Education has lost. Yes, Bob and I had many happy associations. He and his girls, George and I and our son and grandchildren even picked blackberries together. Bob will be sorely missed.

Steve

Steve Willard was born in Stockton, Texas, living there until he went away to college at Sul Ross, Alpine, Texas, where he met Ann. A pre-med student, majoring in Chemistry, Steve graduated in 1951, and he was told that he would not be drafted during the Korean conflict as long as he was in school, but found after one year that he would be...after enrolling at the University of Texas. He and Ann were married on August 25, 1952. After 4 1/2 months at Camp Chaffee, Arkansas, he was assigned to Japan for 1 1/2 years, returning home in May, 1954. Bill Wolfe at the University of Texas wrote his superiors of the shortage of SPE teachers, and the Red Cross helped him to be discharged 3 months early.

Steve became an EMR teacher at San Angelo, Texas, then taught an elementary EMR group for one year; Lakeview School System asked if he would start their program, and he did the screening and evaluation. Ann taught at the same schools Steve did. Steve got his master's degree in 1958, and went to Northwestern State Teacher's College, Louisiana, becoming the educational diagnostician of a team of four, including a psychiatric social worker, psychologist, and diagnostician; he later became the chairman of the team. Everybody was urged to have an Ed.S. or Ph.D. so he went to Virginia in 1967 where he received his degree in 1969; his master's had been in Physical Handicaps and his doctorate in Mental Retardation. Returning to college proved somewhat a disappointment, because the stress of being first the boss, then a student, bothered him.

Steve joined the U of A faculty in July 1969, working with Gale Lambright the last part of the summer before she and Dr. Harvey left, he to replace Bill Wolfe who was to "move up". This did not happen, and Dr. Harvey spent his time at the University of Texas on a professorship, but not as chairman of the department. Gale went to the University of South Alabama and Wilson Dietrich returned from CDLD to become head of the department at U of A. At the university, Steve was on soft money, and with federal grants being reduced, the future of Hackberry was uncertain. According to Ann, uncertainty always "got to" Steve, and she feels that trauma plays a great part in predisposing one to cancer.

In 1972, on the way to CEC in Washington, Steve was forced to leave the airport and stay overnight at a hotel in Atlanta, suffering from severe stomach cramps. He called Ann to get him a doctor's appointment, but did go on to CEC first. He was convinced he had an ulcer, and the medication for that ailment helped for three days. At night he would have terrible stomach cramps, and his stomach was swollen but he was still going to work and doing his teaching. Ann was at Special Olympics at Thomas Field on the UA campus when he called to say the doctor was putting him in the hospital. A blockage was found in the lower intestine and exploratory surgery scheduled; at 7:00 p.m. that night, Dr. Fitts performed a colostomy and said that Steve would never return to work, and could live only eighteen months to two years. There was widespread cancer with the liver already affected, and Fitts said that cobalt could not be used on the liver, but he would send Steve and Ann anywhere they chose. Dr. Fitts called Houston for advice, and Steve was given chemotherapy for two weeks at a time, with two weeks off. He came home after the first chemotherapy but not enough pain killer could be administered there so after three days he returned to the hospital, where phlebitis developed. He was home again for one weekend, but his medication was producing hallucinations. He had to be placed, strapped down, in a security room for two days to prevent his hurting himself, and even Ann could not go in. He died in May, 1972.

Money donated to the Stephen A. Willard Memorial provides an annual plaque to the undergraduate Special Education student who has shown more than just academic achievement, but who also shares empathy with, general understanding of, and ability to work with children. Bobby Wyatt was the first recipient, and his own daughter, Sharon, was one. Since Dr. Elliott came, Ann Willard has been invited to present the plaque.

Tommy

Professor and MR Program Chairperson

This boss of mine—as department head of the Area of Mental Retardation—dates back further than any bosses except Dr. Harvey and George. We had at least one course together at the graduate level back in 1960, and have many things in common, having attended the same colleges—Livingston State Teacher's College, where we met our mates—, and to the University of Alabama. Tommy is even a native of Walker County as is George, and we both have farming as a hobby, which can get to be more like work sometimes—but it is still fun.

After receiving advanced degrees, he went to Panama City, Florida, as coordinator of Special Education, where he remained until he joined the faculty at the University of Alabama in 1968. When he came I was already there as coordinator of clinical experiences but, as the department grew, I worked in that capacity in the area of Mental Retardation. We shared an office and students, problems and joys.

He says, "The MR Program which I coordinate continues to be the largest program in the area of special education in terms of faculty, research funds (generated from outside sources), student enrollment and student graduates at the Bachelor's, Master's, Ed.S./AA, and Doctoral level.

As an active member of the Teacher Education Division, Council for Exceptional Children, at both the national and state levels, I attend all of their workshops that travel will permit. I also supervise student teachers and interns in public schools on a weekly basis and directing a Sunday School department and a summer program for Children and Youth with Mental Handicaps helps to keep me abreast of current practices in the classroom."

Dr. Tommy Russell is and has been for a long time a true professional leader, having held positions of responsibility in both education and special education organizations in Alabama and in Florida as well as at the national level. He has received numerous awards including a 1986 resolution of commendation from the Alabama State House of Representatives for his distinguished service, the Alpha Brown Award in 1981 for meritorious service to exceptional children, and the University of Alabama Alumni's Commitment to Teaching Award in 1979.

One of the great pleasures in my life has been to know Tommy and Allene through these years, to see Special Education grow as it has, and to learn together. Tommy is one of the finest Christian gentlemen I know and countless students through the years feel the same as I do. His letter at the time of my retirement summarizes our years together.

Dear Daisy,

Never did we realize that hot summer of 1960 in Dr. Bedwell's Arts and Crafts for Atypical Children that the day could come when you would retire, with all your energy, vivaciousness, and ability to motivate fellow graduate students. We could not understand how you could go to school all day, go to the park for two hours of volleyball, spend the rest of the night canning and freezing vegetables, and then be fresh as a "Daisy" the next morning. Truly, your friendship and wise counsel has meant much to us both over the years. We just hope that our years and contributions to exceptional children will have the deep impact that your years of dedication and professional service have had on exceptional children and youth in Alabama, and we hope that you will continue to visit us and keep us posted on your many activities. We are sure that you are not really retiring but simply accepting new challenges and responsibilites, whatever they may be. We will always wish for you and your family many happy years together doing the many exciting things you enjoy participating in. The Russells will always cherish your friendship.

Sincerely,
Tommy and Allene

Bill

Bill did not know when he gave each faculty member a desk calendar for 1974-75 that it would contribute to a book someday, but most of the quotations placed at the beginning of my chapters came from it, since there was one at the top of each week. It turned out to be my final appointment book, and I have kept it in order to remind me that I once led an organized, disciplined life.

Dr. William Heller came to the University of Alabama as department head in 1971 from the Bureau of Education for the Handicapped, and during his days as area chairman from 1971 to 1973 much progress was made. The undergraduate program was begun, grant programs were increased, and work was continued with Partlow and Bryce. There were valuable inroads made in the treatment of women and blacks, and many efforts were undertaken with public school systems—including those in Hale, Greene, and Walker Counties—to assist in the in-service and credit courses made available to their teachers. In fact, the success of that particular program brought distinction to the whole department, and to the University as a whole. The College of Education, in 1974, received one of five special National Awards for Distinguished Achievement during the annual convention of the American Association of Colleges for Teacher Education, held in Chicago, Illinois. The award was presented to Dean Paul G. Orr and Dr. Heller in recognition of the quality of the Reality Oriented Teacher Education Program (R.O.T.E).

Bill left us to become admisistrator of Byrce Hospital, and today he is Dean of the College of Education and Allied Professions at the University of North Carolina. His duties include supervision of two ROTC units, the teaching of Special Education courses, and serving as chairman of the CEC Professional Affairs Committee. In the spring of 1982, he taught a resource LD and MH class at West Charlotte High School five periods a day while still serving as dean.

All of his faculty does this in order not to lose touch with the public schools.

There are many examples I could give in order to demonstrate Bill's extraordinary level of human understanding, but one prime display occurred at a CEC meeting in New York when he insisted that I use his return plane ticket to come home early for the funeral of my bother-in-law while he arranged to ride home in a car with students. Bill and I will recall our professional association with nothing but pleasure.

State of Alabama
DEPARTMENT OF MENTAL HEALTH
BRYCE HOSPITAL
Tuscaloosa, Alabama 35401

February 5, 1976

Dear Daisy,

It is hard to believe that there is going to be an Area of Special Education without a Daisy at the Unversity of Alabama. After all, you were certainly one of the mainstays across the years of the program and served as the thread that tied it all together from the Harvey days through the Heller days. Needless to say, in my opinion, the strength of that thread was extremely strong, and I did appreciate on many occasions the fact that you were there.

I guess one of the things that always amazed me most was how many people you knew by their first names in Alabama and especially in the Tuscaloosa area. And not only did you know the first names of the parents but you could trace right down through the siblings almost to the name of the youngest child in the family. I don't know how you did it, but it never ceased to amaze me.

I was also fascinated by your organization regarding child rearing. Not too many people can be grandparents and at the same time be parents and do it legitimately without divorce, etc. involved but, by George, you did it.

Another thing I know I will miss, and all of the Department will miss, is the fine cookin' that you so graciously provided on a number of occasions. As you know, my stomach has a high priority and seldom was it any more satisfied than when it was involved with interacting with some of the Daisy Styles' Southern cookin'. In fact, I never found much that you weren't somehow involved in—cookin', grandparents, CEC, plants and flowers, in addition to being a good wife and mother. I am certain most of our students who had an opportunity to spend time with you have had their lives enriched considerably, and I would suspect that if they threw a testimonial for you, one-half of the present teachers in Alabama would come because you have touched them in some way or another. For you, as a special educator and a teacher educator, I am most grateful and I am certain that the State of Alabama likewise owes you a great deal of gratitude.

I do indeed find it kind of hard to imagine special education without an actively involved Daisy Styles. However, I also know that Daisy Styles, even in retirement, will be involved to the so-called "hilt". I do hope, however, that you will take every opportunity to enjoy the richly deserved retirement which you and George have earned and share it together as you often indicated to me you would.

My very best to you, and if you ever need a friend for whatever the situation, please know you can always call on me. My very best personal regards always.

Your friend,
Harold W. Heller
Hospital Superintendent

George

What can I say about my husband George, the principal who survived me longer than all my other bosses combined? From 1947 until 1963, he was my principal at Searles and Cottondale Schools. That back road to Cottondale is still one we enjoy driving over, because it recalls those happy years of heading out to work early after we had dropped Shirley and George off at Mrs. Norman Luker's, where they would walk to the old Alberta School on fifteenth street, and return each afternoon to meet us. That first year George was just five so he spent his days there. Shirley says Jerry, a first grader also, would run off and leave her because he was afraid someone would call her his "girl friend." Betty, his sister, was one of my first "gifted" students. Lettie Collins kept them during their pre-school days, except summers when they attended University of Alabama Child Development, and they still say, "Fishy, Fishy in the brook, Papa cot him with a hook; Mama fried him in a pan, Baby et him like a man." She was so good to them!

For George to have endured a wife on a school faculty for so long and still stay married tells you a lot about him. They were extremely happy years—and they were missed when University days came—but never did a semester pass without a student teacher at Cottondale who required frequent supervision!

The following paragraph, taken from the Alabama Elementary Principal's Newsletter, Spring 1985, could have been written about him:

"The principal of a school is its leader, and on the effectiveness of its leader depends the effectiveness of a school. Even though effective principal leadership may be difficult to define, an effective principal usually is not difficult to spot because the gauge of principal effectivedness is the school itself. An effective school is seen as an optimum learning environment - one that nurtures the cognitive, affective, social, aesthetic development of its children and youth. The goal of the principal should be to develop such an environment. The role of the principal encompasses all the functions essential to achieving this goal."

Chapter Three
THE TRUNK

"The great end of life is not knowledge but action."

- Thomas Henry Huxley

No school program ever succeeds unless the parents take an active role, and nowhere is this more evident than in the field of exceptional children. So much of the success of a school depends upon what has taken place in the home prior to the child's admission, as well as upon the continued interest of the parents in the school and its program.

A project undertaken in Walker County during the days of Dr. Heller's leadership provided one of the most tangible evidences of how parents and teachers work together for the educational good of the children. As a part of this project, parents and teachers participated in very informal panel discussions during in-service meetings, and I have included in this chapter the transcript of a tape recording of one such conversation. A great deal of discussion went on beyond the completion of the tape, but much can be learned as these parents speak spontaneously and openly of their concerns with and great interest in their children's education and training.

Following the transcript is a discussion of the valuable work done by the National Association for Retarded Children (NARC) and the Tuscaloosa Association for Retarded Children (TARC), two organizations which, along with the Civitans, have done a great deal to aid retarded children and their parents. Also included is a brief discussion and definition of mental retardation itself, a condition which is shrouded by a great number of misconceptions which hamper the efforts made to deal rationally with the problem.

A Tape On Working With Parents

LIB POWELL: "My child is exceptional. He'll be six years old tomorrow. His name is Robert. He came into a family of old parents. He has a brother who will be twenty and another who will be eleven. As parents, we had to face quite an adjustment, as any family would with children that far apart in ages, and it really made us change our style of life. Because Robert was exceptional, as we found out the day he was born, we had extra adjustments to make. One of the major ones, after we had made ours, was the grandmother. Her first reaction was to hide what had happened under the rug. She wanted to tell my brother and then swear him to secrecy, so we had to straighten her out on this. As for school, he is somewhat a veteran because, in his first six years, he has been to school three years. We are fortunate because The University of Alabama started a pre-school class in February 1970 just before his third birthday; he was one of the first enrolled and remained in it all of his pre-school years. As I think back over those first months in the class, the most valuable experience was to go and observe the teacher work with him. We were asked to go one day each week and stay three hours. This class was in the psychology building and Glenda Willis was the teacher. I felt that this helped me in working with him because I could see how the teacher did many things. She would say, "Does Robert do ____ at home?" I would have to admit I had not even thought over the fact that he might do some tasks for himself. I guess I was really over— protective of him; I recall the times when he was younger that I would lift him into his high chair, and it wasn't until I was on crutches one time that I discovered he could climb up by himself. He had to do it for himself and he did, the first time, and I thought how long I had been doing it for him. Another time, when Marilee and I were talking with Mrs. Styles' class about a year ago and she spoke of Bart's dressing himself, I thought, "You foolish thing! Here you've been dressing Robert all this time and never gave a thought to the fact that he could do some of it for himself." I went home that day, and he could dress himself. It took patience at first to keep hands off. It can be very helpful for a teacher to point out things that we might try.

MARILEE BROWN: We have two children. Bart is seven and one-half, his brother is thirteen months old. Bart is Robert's classmate. Bart is mongoloid due to Down's syndrome. Since he was the first child, and because we wanted a boy so bad, we were both upset at first. I was very fortunate in having the husband I have. He just said, "He's ours and we're going to take him home and love him and raise him." He really straightened me out after I got over feeling sorry for myself. Bart also had a hole in his heart and it really hampered his activity because he would get so out of breath. He could only take two steps and he would have to stop. At four and one-half he had heart surgery. It was just like they wheeled one boy in, and another out. He had so much energy. One of his eyes turned in a little bit, so we got glasses. One of his legs turned outward, so we had surgery on that. When he was two days old, he had a transfusion, and Dr. Reese felt as though an RH incompatability may have caused Bart to have a little cerebral palsy. I went to work in Special Education at the time Dr. Harvey was there, and it was just great for me because there was so much information available. Everybody was so good to talk to me. When the pre-school class was organized, Bart was the first one enrolled. Then seven children were enrolled, Robert being one of them. When Bart finishes this summer, we hope he can go into a resource class this fall, with first grade part of the time, special education the rest. He can write his name and we are so excited about that. He does a lot that I would not have thought he could do. Mrs. Russell suggests games that she thinks would be good for him and many kinds of activities that would help his motor coordination, which is not too good. She told us to get a pencil or crayon and just let him scribble. He wasn't too thrilled with that, but now he says, "I've got to go do my homework, Mother." She has helped us so much and encouraged us and really helped our son.

MRS. STYLES: We now have the mother of a little girl. I didn't mean for it to work out that we had all young children. We also had a daddy until today, but at the last minute he couldn't come.

MARY ALICE JONES: She was late in starting to school. I didn't know there was anything wrong with Dewana but the doctor knew from her birth. At about age six months we asked about her and he told us she was spastic, and he said that it was his first case, so he didn't know what to do. I thought that I could take care of her, so why follow his suggestion and put her in an institution? I checked with Crippled Children's Service. I didn't know anything about the school for handicapped children until Dewana was about six. I put her at Northington. At first I had always tried to treat her as a normal child; she had always seemed to know what to do but just couldn't make her muscles respond so she attempted to imitate the actions of other children. Later, she was in a new class of multiple handicapped children operated by TARC, and just being with other children helped her so much. In swimming, if the water was at all cool, she would tighten up worse. If I would see them try to do things with her I knew she couldn't do, I would want to say something, but I would hold back.

MRS. STYLES: I know all of you are going to think of many questions. I can already think of dozens of things I want to ask you.

JOE POWELL: How many other children you have?

MRS. JONES: Dewana is an only child, but she loves all children. She does drool, and sticks her tongue out a lot, so other children do notice that. I have a brother just younger than she is, and she has a lot of cousins all of whom fuss about who is going to wipe her mouth. My brother is the only one who puts up a fuss about that, but she is winning him around. He just doesn't want us to know how much he likes her.

MRS. STYLES: Interrupt us at any time. I thought we would let my mother tell us about her work with parents at the Hackberry program, and then we would talk a little about work with parents, and how we as teachers can share our knowledge with parents.

Q: Mrs. Powell, how do your other children react to Robert?

MRS. POWELL: Richard, now eleven, was just six when Robert was born, and he had been the baby of the family all that time. He showed some noraml resentment and didn't like all the time we spent with Robert. The older one we told immediately that Robert was mongoloid, and he has been marvelous in working with him. There is a relationship between those two that you don't often find between brothers. There is enough difference between their ages that Milton can pick at him, and do many things to help with him. Robert is a cheerful child and gets the silly giggles at times. He hadn't done that until this week at school, but Mrs. Russell says she sees now what I mean. Everything was funny at nap time. Now that Richard is older, he is very accepting of Robert. We did not tell him for a couple of years that Robert was retarded and we had to gradually let him see that Robert is much slower at things than the average child. Richard loves to play with him now; in fact, one of the games he loves to play comes while putting Robert to bed, and the younger boy resists. Richard will say, "Come here, Robert. There's a tiger in your bed!" Robert will come running and say, "He got away."

JOE POWELL: Bart was six and one-half when your second child was born. What kinds of fears did you have during your pregnancy?

MRS. BROWN: I didn't really have much time to let anybody else know. And we were so excited and wanted another child so badly. That overruled the apprehension and I knew that worry wasn't going to help me.

MRS. STYLES: I know what you mean because we had our last child in our 40's. George had taken course work in special education before I did. We breathed a sigh of relief many times and said, "Thank goodness, we already have our family." In fact, an obstetrician had told us nearly twenty years before that I would never carry a child to full term after a miscarriage with twins, so I had somewhat the same feelings Marilee did. Anybody can worry himself to death, if he really wants to, about anything. Today I realize that my "normal" children could have an automobile or motorcycle accident, football injury, or a fall down the stairs; a million things could make them or me a brain— injured individual. Marilee, would you advise any parent of one exceptional child, in cases where there has been any research to indicate the possibility of inherited or chromosome disorders, to have studies made ahead?

MRS. BROWN: By all means.

MRS. STYLES: And teachers need to know what is available and tell parents.

MRS. BROWN: Yes, we didn't know, but our pediatrician did. She had worked at Partlow and knew the work of Sara and Wayne Finley in Birmingham on genetic studies. They are so great, so nice to you. It made us feel so good, and also relieves guilt feelings because any parent of an exceptional child feels, "What did I do that

~~caused this?" This child is a part of them, and if he's not perfect,~~ they feel to blame.

Q: How expensive is it?

A: They cost $50.00 each. I learned later that was half price because of being University connected, and UAB is a part of the University system. Actually that's super low because so much is done. Some of the cost must be covered by federal grants.

Q: I really am glad to find that out. My brother wanted chromosome studies done, and he was told it would cost a thousand dollars.

A: Oh no!

MRS. BROWN: I think our insurance may have paid for some. I really don't know.

Q: Does your doctor have to make the arrangements, or can you do it yourself?

MRS. BROWN: I think you can do it yourself.

MRS. STYLES: This is the first time I have ever really known any specifics about chromosome studies, and we, as teachers, ought to know about these things. So often we are in the closest contact with parents wanting to know where to go for all kinds of help. There are so many free pamphlets, like these I have brought today, that answer some of these questions; I pick them up all the time from Social Security, the Health Department, insurance companies, the March of Dimes, and from Easter Seals. Through the years I have been asked questions, many times by a family about to move to another state and wanting to know what facilities are there. We may not know the specific answer, but we ought to be able to direct parents to sources of information. Dr. Harvey always impressed me so with his knowledge along this line; he was never too busy to talk to a parent. Most recently, on a long-distance call, I was asked if I knew of any tour groups that took along a blind person and made adaptations for the blindness. I could only tell the woman that to accompany a sighted person was the only way I knew it could be done. I had heard that, years ago, railroads gave free fare to a sighted person traveling with a blind one, but I never verified this. We haven't been at it long, but we ought to be able to direct parents to sources of help.

MRS. BROWN: I recently heard of a case in which samples of blood were sent by bus to Birmingham and the people didn't even have to go for their chromosome studies. That might be helpful for those who don't have transportation.

MRS. POWELL: We also had chromosome studies done on Robert, not that we expected at our age to have more children, but for the sake of our other two boys. We thought that if there was anything hereditary, his brothers needed to know it before they had children. Ours was like Marilee's, not hereditary.

MRS. STYLES: There is still so much we don't know about exceptionalities. Some are hereditary, some not. Diabetes, for instance, can causes problems. In our diabetic family, it might have been wise for us to have been careful and not marry someone who is also diabetic (Laughter). What would you do if you are already married, or in love? If you should find some fairly high possibilities, then at least you could decide to adopt a child, or take the chance with a little more knowledge so that maybe it doesn't come as quite as much of a shock to you and doesn't have so many question marks. Mama, is there anything you'd like to add about your three summers as housemother with the Hackberry Program with physically handicapped children?

MRS. MADARIS: I was the first housemother to work with these children. I really enjoyed it, but I was like you; my heart went out to them and I wanted to do everything I could for them, but I soon learned that they were there to learn to do everything they could for themselves. I am also the grandmother of an exceptional child. Our third year, we didn't let the parents come, because we saw how much easier it was to train them alone. You know how mothers are. We were surprised to see how much the children could do for themselves. I would be up with them off and on all night, and if they were sick, we had to call Dr. Reese, or get Dr. Harvey, Dr. Lambright, or Dr. Dietrich. When they spoke of taking them swimming, I had to go to the natatorium and see that for myself. Of course, many had to be taken out of wheelchairs, but everybody went swimming and it was amazing how their muscles would relax when they got in the water. Marvin learned to swim the first summer and could swim two laps of the pool, even though he had never even been allowed to get in a pool before. That just goes to show how many things the kids can learn if just given the opportunity. As grandparents and parents, we give in to them so easily. At first, we would be told at the table, "I don't like that," but they soon learned to take just a little food on their plates and try it. Many who didn't like milk learned to drink it when told how it could help their bones and teeth, and they learned that no tea or coke would be given at times when milk was the beverage. We had to be firm with them. We had no eating problems before summer was over. It was wonderful. We had to take the children up and down the stairs. I remember one day finding Anthony, who was cerebral palsied, climbing down the fire escape, just to prove that he could. Some of the men met him half way and let him climb on down. In the afternoons, after a morning of academics, there would be planned recreation in the yard, and I saw those crippled children play softball, tag, and all other kinds of games, and have so much fun. They had to learn to throw balls. I can remember years back when a child with a disability was kept out of sight, and now so many can make their own way with the help you are giving them.

MRS. POWELL: Speaking of grandmothers, we have had the experience of a grandmother in the house until last Tuesday, when she had to move to a nursing home. She was so much more over-protective even than we were. She would feed our child ice cream, and we would just have to make her mad and tell her to put the spoon down and let him feed himself, and he would. She didn't want him climbing or swimming. If we put his clothes out for him to dress, she would go dress him. We can tell so much difference in his independence just these few days since she has been gone.

MRS. STYLES: There are some important factors to remember in working with parents. You should get to know your parents before any problem arises, so that a conference with the teacher or a visit does not mean that there is automatically trouble. I realize that it gets harder and harder to find the time to do these things. Maybe you get to know your parents better here in Walker County than we do in Tuscaloosa. Do they come to PTA much? No!

MRS. STYLES: What do we do at PTA? We either stand up and be counted by classes to see who won the attendance prize, or sign in on sheets so that everybody who comes can look right there and see who are the ones for Mrs. Styles' special class. Let's face it!

Still not many parents want to publicly say, "Look, I have an exceptional child!"

JOE POWELL: Mrs. Powell, how did you go about convincing the grandmother that you shouldn't hide the fact of an exceptional child?

MRS. POWELL: Well, we just told her flatly from the beginning that we're not going to hide it, because he's a part of the family, and she caught on very quickly. I remember one Christmas when we put pictures of family members on the card and she didn't want Robert included. She had grown up in a time when you did hide a child like this away. I could see that visitors who came that first few weeks were hesitant about the subject, so we made a point of bringing it up ourselves. They were sympathetic and interested. The grandmother was with us about three weeks after Robert was born and she saw that it was best to be open.

Q: How do you get parents to be open about it and admit their child is exceptional? You have to get them to admit it before you can work with them.

MRS. POWELL: I'll have to tell you a story on myself. Robert was a pretty baby. The other two were ugly, though they have outgrown it. The doctor told us his mongoloid characteristics would show up more as he grew older, so I began to fool myself and say, "He doesn't really look that much different," I had done a pretty good job of convincing myself that maybe, just maybe, everything was all right.

One day downtown a teenage boy stopped me and said, "How old is your baby? I have a little brother who is mongoloid." I had to really laugh at myself because here was a teenager who recognized Down's syndrome better than I did. There is sort of a security in trying to fool yourself. I don't know the answer.

MRS. STYLES: I'm sure part of the answer is to get those parents involved at the child's preschool level. You teachers have probably found, as I did, that to have a teenager diagnosed as retarded for the first time and suggest special class placement is almost impossible. I really have serious doubts about any good that it may do to place a child at that age for the first time. I will probably get fired for saying this, but I almost feel that if they can't be diagnosed and placed no later than first, second, or third grade, you had just about forget it. Resource type classes with more emphasis on vocational areas like shop and home economics, and with good association in normal peer groups, just may be far better than self-contained classes. Of course, I realize there are problems both ways. Some of my students who have gone on to junior high—and are just as pretty and cute as the other girls with their mini-skirts and make-up— quite often come back to cry on my shoulder about the problems they face and about their lack of acceptance. I don't know the answers and am not going to live long enough to know, but I hope some of you someday will do research on success related to different ages of placement.

TEACHER: I involve my parents in parties, field trips.

ANOTHER TEACHER: If you can ever get them to come and visit the class, it helps!

MRS. STYLES: I'm sure none of you fit this category, but you know, I've seen teachers who have the feeling that the last thing they want is to have the parents visit. Children many times are more excitable, and that's sad. I don't recall that I ever felt free to visit my own children's classes much more than for maybe one prescribed hour during American Education week. And my children really, especially at the high school level, would not always give us PTA notices, because they would be afraid we might discuss them with their teachers. You can really get a guilty feeling about going and taking up some teacher's time, and that's not good, but in special education, I would hope that parents are made to feel welcome. We made things—sock puppets, for instance—for Halloween Carnival, and I learned how helpful it was to have parents come and help. It was so good to just have them sitting around, free to talk, and to see that other people faced many of the same things they faced. I can remember someone saying at Opportunity School (TARC) that a little fifteen-year old mother burst out crying one day when she realized there were other handicapped children just like hers. She had felt that hers was the only case in the world. She was at a beauty shop at the time, and heard another mother speak of her child. There are so many new things coming out all the time. I believe in Tuscaloosa we have just had three Sickle Cell Anemia workshops. I had three places to be those afternoons so didn't get to go, but we ought to learn all we can and read as much as possible. Testing of PKU is now routinely done in all cases at birth. There are so many advances.

Q: I'd like to know how you got your pre-school classes; it seems that we have to fight for everything we get. We have to take ours to another area.

MRS. STYLES: Alabama has much legislation concerning handicapped children and preschool classes. Much of it at the present time is permissive but will likely get to be mandatory more and more. If your system is interested enough to allot some of their designated pre-school units for handicapped children, they may. I believe the law is such that for each ten units at preschool level, one must be for handicapped children. Some of ours were established for research purposes, but we did have to pay some at first. Much of what has been accomplished has come through the efforts of parent-groups. The National Association for Retarded Children (now Citizens) has spearheaded so much of what has come about. I have always tried to put myself in the place of parents, and felt that, no matter how the statistics reported it, my one case would be treated just as though it were 100%. I would want my child to have public school services that all children receive as far as possible.

Q: I often used qualified parents as substitutes. How do you feel about this?

MRS. STYLES: I often tell my students, if it works, do it. If it doesn't, try something else. I happen to know that it works beautifully having Mrs. Jones at Northington as an aide. In other cases, as Mama mentioned at Hackberry, sometimes more can be accomplished without them. For some, who have had full time care of a seriously involved child, the break works wonders. Our parents should always know we are interested and will help them to work out their problems in every way possible.

Q: I have a seventeen-year-old CP in my class and as yet I cannot find one thing he can do on his own. Have any of you found this?

MRS. STYLES: Can he even use one finger?

A: He's getting more and more involved. I don't believe he's getting any therapy. He is of normal intelligence, and he could learn to read, but his mother has a big family, and she doesn't have time to turn the pages for him.

MRS. STYLES: I was in a class yesterday of all wheelchair young people and at least half of them were typing, some with only one finger. I would check in Birmingham, and Tuscaloosa. Dr. Loreta Holder would be able to help about where to go for help. If the child really can't do anything, I am not at all sure that the family is doing him or themselves a favor by keeping him at home. There are many good centers where he might get more help. Film—strips, tape recordings, or remote control devices, there should be some devices or ways for him to learn. Don't stop until all possible sources are exhausted. Check with Vocational Rehabilitation; its purpose is for vocational training and should be able to help you. Many agencies are available for help. The surplus war center at Attalla, which provides things for school use, is a good source of inexpensive equipment—typewriters, for instance. I believe that's where we got a tractor for gardening. My blind friend told me that the Foundation for the Blind also provides talking books and record players for the physically handicapped, free, through any public library.

We have seen today, as teachers and parents, our need to make each other aware of the services available, and we need to understand each other and work together. The earlier we get involved, the better. When you people first had a pre-school group, how often did you meet?

A: Once a week, sometimes for two or three hours. And nearly 100% attendance.

(The tape ended but discussion continued.)

The following section deals with the NARC, with local organizations, and with the definition of mental retardation.

The National Association for Retarded Children, located in New York, and founded in 1950, has over 950 member associations in forty-nine states composed of parents and others interested in mental retardation. The NARC program is based on the demonstrated fact that retarded children can be helped, and it calls for a number of measures, including diagnostic clinics, home visiting programs, parent counseling, nursery classes, day care centers, residence centers, special schooling and training geared to the degree of the handicap, religious education, recreation facilities, vocational training centers, sheltered workshops and placement services for adults who need employment, protection and guardianship as required, and research into the causes of retardation.

The NARC stimulates local, state, and federal action on behalf of these programs, helps initiate pilot and demonstration projects, maintains a staff of consultants in such areas as education, nursing, and rehabilitation, publishes materials, and acts as a central information resource, and referral agency. The NARC Research Fund sponsors studies at leading universities which, along with those being carried on by the federal government and other private foundations, are uncovering more of the means of preventing and the amelioration of mental retardation. Grants from the fund are made upon recommendations of a Scientific Research Advisory Board composed of prominent people from the biological and social sciences. The initiation of this board resulted in a survey sponsored by NARC to develop a sound basis on which research could be developed; the survey was published in 1958 in a volume called *Mental Subnormality*, by Drs. Richard L. Masland, Seymour B. Sarason, and Thomas Gladwin.

National Retarded Children's Week is held each November to draw attention to the national problem of mental retardation and its effect on the family, the community, and the economy. Each year the observance concludes on Thanksgiving Day in appreciation of the forward strides being made in improving the chances for the mentally retarded to lead happy, useful, and satisfying lives, and in anticipation of future gains. The special week serves as a period when many of the NARC units raise funds in local communities to carry on the needed services and to underwrite research.

No one can adequately describe the social and moral forces which cause the formation of community groups and promote programs for the general welfare of a community; however, once such groups are formed the purpose of the group is usually defined and the course of action outlined. During the fall of 1956, a group composed of parents and friends of retarded children began a series of meetings in private homes to discuss the needs of the children in the Tuscaloosa area whose condition of mental retardation restricted their horizons for development in the customary manner, and from these meetings the Tuscaloosa Association for Retarded Children was born. This orgaization was formed to promote the general welfare of retarded children by helping organize parent groups, counseling and advising parents in their problems associated with retarded children, supporting state and national legislation of benefit to retarded children, disseminating information to inform the general public of the problem, to encourage the training and education of personnel to work in the field of mental retardation, and to raise funds and otherwise contribute to the accomplishment of these purposes.

In the fall of 1957 the first campaign for funds to operate the Tuscaloosa Opportunity School for Exceptional Children was undertaken and the Opportunity School began operation. Initially only one teacher was employed and the capacity of the school was approximately 10 children. A building was rented on the Northington Campus and renovated to house the school. Mr. J. M. Armstrong, Sr. was the first president of TARC and spark-plugged the fund drive and organization of the Opportunity School. By the fall of 1958 the school had grown to approximately twice the original size and two teachers were employed. Rev. B. W. Allen was president of TARC for the year of 1958-1959. TARC joined the United Fund during 1959 and participated in the 1959 United Fund Campaign for funds.

By the beginning of the 1959 fall term of school the needs of the community for the Opportunity School were crowding the facilities of the school and the plans for a new highway threatened to destroy the building housing the Opportunity School. Plans for expansion began under the guidance of William J. Williamson, Jr. A new building was located and a move was planned. Money with which to renovate the new building was not part of the budget, but necessity required the move. A major contribution of material and work was made by the Tuscaloosa Jaycettes, the Civitans contributed substantially, and the United Fund of Tuscaloosa County, in support of its principle of no solicitations except the United Campaign, supplied the remaining funds. The new school facilities were ready for occupancy in February, 1960.

The following activities are offered at the Opportunity School: a pre-school program for educable-trainable children in the two and a half to six years of age range; an activity program for children over twenty-one; a program in speech therapy; a mother's club for mothers of all retarded children, regardless of age; a testing program administered by the Psychology and Special Education departments at the University of Alabama; monthly meetings of the Tuscaloosa Association for Retarded Children.

It is impossible to give credit to the many oranizations and individuals who have given freely and generously of their time and their moral and financial support to the projects and goals of the Tuscaloosa Association for Retarded Children. TARC could have accomplished nothing without their help. It takes nothing from our gratitude and appreciation to point out the sound economy in training our mentally retarded to become at least partially self-supporting and self-reliant instead of another statistic in a state-supported institution. The value of this support in terms of meeting the emotional needs of the children and their parents and friends is beyond estimation.

It is important as well that we clearly establish what we mean by the term, "mental retardation," and what some of the consequences of this terrible affliction are, especially since there seem to be so many misconceptions. Simply stated, mental retardation is a condition resulting from a basic abnormality of the human mind, and involves a lack of intellectual ability resulting from arrested mental development. Mental retardation interferes with the ability to adjust to the demands of the environment, and manifests itself in poor learning, inadequate social adjustment, and delayed achievement. Usually this condition is either present at birth or begins during childhood.

Among the common misconceptions of mental retardation is that the retarded look different than the rest of us, that they are mentally ill or insane, or that there should be some stigma attached to the family of a retarded person—even though heredity has proven to be the most negligible contributing cause. Mental retardation is not a disease; rather, it is a symptom of an injury, of some obscure failure of development, or even of an inadequate opportunity to learn. Just as a fever is a symptom of an infection, mental retardation is a sympton of mongolism, birth injury or infection, or even of inadequate stimulation in childhood. It can be so severe that the afflicted person never leaves protective care, or so mild that it is detected only under stress or through special tests. In most instances, retardation can be clearly distinguished from mental illness, for mental illness strikes and incapacitates after there has been normal development up to the time of the affliction. The younger the child the more difficult it is to distinguish between the two; however, accurate diagnosis is an essential prelude to treatment. Unfortunately, the present limitations to our knowledge in this field make this diagnosis extremely difficult when the very young are involved.

More than 100 causes for mental retardation are known, and many others are suspected. Mental retardation results when there is incomplete development or destruction of tissues of the central nervous system. Sometimes the brain does not develop before birth. Overexposure to X-rays, certain illnesses, infections, and glandular disorders during pregnancy may result in a child's being retarded. Extraordinarily prolonged labor, pelvic pressure, hemorrage, or lack of oxygen may injure the baby's brain, and a child's full mental development may be arrested after birth by an accident, poisoning, glandular disturbances, chemical imbalance, or childhood diseases. Recent research also points to severe early emotional deprivation and other cultural and environmental factors as causes of mental retardation.

Mental retardation stemming from certain causes can be prevented. Some instances of chemical imbalance that cause serious damage to the brain can now be controlled by special diet or drugs. When tests show that parents' blood types are incompatible, immediate blood transfusions can by given to the infant, and a pregnant woman can be vigilant to avoid exposure to infection that may cause her baby to be retarded. In a few disorders, early surgery may eliminate sources of pressure on the developing brain. Through research now under way, it is hoped that the causes of retardation will be more precisely broken down and more of them eliminated.

Another common misunderstanding involving mental retardation is that children of lower classes are most aften the victims of this condition. While cultural factors may indeed play a role, there is no way to know ahead of time which children will prove to be mentally retarded. Such children are born to average, brilliant, and dull parents, and into both highly-educated and illiterate families. All racial, religious, social, economic, and national groups are affected.

As far as the prognosis for mental retardation, we know that with proper help and special schooling, twenty-five out of thirty retarded children can be educated in the basic skills of reading, writing, and arithmetic, and can be gainfully employed as adults in unskilled and semi-skilled work. Four more out of every thirty can be trained to take care of personal needs, and many of them can go on to do simple tasks at home, or at work in sheltered workshops; as adults they will be semi-dependent. One out of every thirty individuals, though, will require care around the clock throughout their lives.

Chapter Four

THE ROOTS

"Success isn't a result of spontaneous combustion. You must set yourself on fire."

-Arnold H. Glassow

When one speaks of "the roots" of education for the exceptional child in the state of Alabama, one must make mention of the life and work of the late Mrs. Alpha Brown, who came to the Alabama State Department of Education in 1956 as Chief Consultant for Special Education. Therefore, I have begun this section with an important address which Alpha delivered to a group of teachers of exceptional children in Huntsville, Alabama, in 1972. Also included is some of the history of the organization founded by Mrs. Brown in 1957, the Alabama State Teachers of Exceptional Children, as well as some of the tributes offered to Mrs. Brown at the time of her retirement in 1969.

"It is difficult to trace the history of the program for exceptional children from its beginning. The first record we find of any service to exceptional children is on a 1937 W.P.A. payroll which lists five hospital teachers. In 1941 there was a special Federal grant for cerebral palsied children, and through this grant, classes for spastic children were begun in Brimingham, and classes for all types of crippled children were begun in Mobile. The board of education furnished the teachers, and the grant money was used for equipment, maid service, some physical and speech therapy, braces, wheelchairs, and scholarships for teachers. In the Birmingham classes the children were selected on a rotating basis; the children were brought from all over the state for a six-month stay, and at the end of that period, the group was sent home and another group brought in. As you can see, this was a boarding school (Charlanne School). In Mobile, there were day classes. Parents did not want this service limited to six months, so they began to discuss the advisability of having these classes at home, and this led into classes at the local level.

"Day classes for blacks were started at the same time in Birmingham under this Federal grant, and two black teachers were sent to Michigan for training. After they had been there one semester, a black teacher from New Jersey entered the school to get training because her superintendent wanted to start the first handicapped class for blacks, and she was surprised to learn that such classes were already underway in Alabama.

"In 1951, the Legislature appropriated $25,000 under Act 636, passed in September 1951 for physically handicapped children, but the law didn't make explicit how the funds were to be handled. The Attorney General, the legislators who introduced the bill, and others were consulted, and it was decided that the Crippled Children's Service would handle the money and use it for equipment and special services. The teachers were furnished by the State Board of Education. Each month the money was decided according to enrollment, with ten the required number; if eight were on the roll, one month in one class, the class received four-fifths of the full amount for a class for that month. Each class received about $15.00 per child per month. In 1953, Act 653 was passed, giving $50,000 for physically handicapped classes, and that year there were forty-eight such classes in Alabama, located in Mobile, Birmingham, Huntsville, Gadsden, Anniston, Decatur, and Tuscaloosa.

"In 1955, the Legislature passed Act 249 relating to the education of exceptional children, a bill considered by experts to be one of the best in the country. Flexible and broad in scope, it provided for all the needed equipment, services, and instructional material; however, not enough money was allocated. The act authorized the State Board of Education, on the recommendation of the State Superintendent of Education, to extablish rules and regulations relating to the allocation of funds, certification of teachers, size of classes, eligibility of pupils to receive instruction, training and experience required for professional personnel other than teachers and other regulations which are necessary to the effective operation of an educational program for exceptional children. It authorized the employment of qualified supervisory personnel in the State Department of Education and expenditure of the minimum program funds and local school funds for the education of exceptional children.

"I came to the State Department of Education in 1956, one year after the act was passed. For the first seven years, the Special Education staff consisted of me and a half-time secretary. I found that very few people understood Special Education, and even though this lack of understanding was expected because the program was new in Alabama, many, many, problems arose.

"There was some misunderstanding about the financing of the program, since there were no special appropriations at first. Later the Trainable Mentally Retarded received a special appropriation of $300,000, which was eventually increased to $306,000. This program is a part of the Minimum Program Fund and is financed like the regular program, with the only difference being that the Special Class Unit is based on enrollment rather than daily attendance. With Special Education, the minimum required enrollment for physically handicapped is eight and ten for Mentally Retarded. Later, Federal appropriations helped with the expenses but not with teachers' salaries.

"Housing was another problem. I will give three examples, though there are many more. After a special class started, there was no room, and it is impossible to provide a quality program of Special Education in crowded quarters. There was no room for equipment, materials for instruction, group work, etc. One class was housed on the back porch of the teacher's home, and when I visited, she had her apron on and was doing her housework, I believe, while her pupils were coloring. This was soon changed or the unit would have been cancelled. Another class was housed in the back corner of the hall, with no partition to separate the class from the regular pupils who frequently ran back and forth. I don't know how the teacher heard the pupils or vice versa; all the children could do was sit, because there was no room to move around. This was soon changed. Later, we required that Special

Classes be held in regular classroom buildings with pupils of the same chronological age, and now, in each building or new school constructed, plans are made for the exceptional children.

"We insisted the school day be the same as the regular school day unless a doctor told us that the pupils could only attend so many hours a day. If some of the pupils needed additional breaks, it was permitted. We thought these classes should be an integrated part of the school system. Once a year we required a progress report from each teacher, and one year we asked them to list the ways in which they participated; thirty-three different ways were listed. One teacher organized her class into a serving club, another into a sewing club. If a student ripped a seam or hem, lost a button or any minor thing, her class repaired it. They were members of the Glee Club, took part in the Science Fair, mimeographed school materials, etc.

"We recommended a sequence of Special Education classes, as a long-range goal, at the primary, elementary, and high school levels, with a student to be promoted from one special class to another every three to four years. Some systems would have enough classes to promote every year. Some superintendents wouldn't start a program of Special Education unless there could be two units, one class at the elementary level and one at the high school level; this way they had a place for the pupils in the elementary class to go when they became too old or too large for the elementary class.

"Until the school year 1962-63, all that was required for the establishment of a Special Class were some children, a teacher, and a place for them to sit, and some of our classes were good. In 1962-63, however before a pupil was placed in a Special class, he had to be evaluated. A regular teacher could not take a pupil from her class who was a discipline problem, an attendance problem, or for some reason, didn't fit into her class and say to the teacher, 'He's yours.' The Special Class teacher could tell her that she couldn't take him until he was evaluated. This is an expensive program and we want people placed in the right places. The ones who don't belong lose ground, and the ones who do belong don't get enough of what they need, so both suffer.

"We asked each superintendent to appoint a committee an admission and dismissal composed of three disciplines: medicine, psychology, and education. These committees would review this material and recommend those who qualified for the class, and in this way, no one factor or no one person determined placement. We thought that the eligibility material, psychological and medical tests, social history, and school record belonged in a confidential file, housed in the building where the class was housed, not in the superintendent's office 10 or 15 miles away. The teacher needs to study these files in planning her work with each child.

"In 1959 the State Superintendent of Education appointed a State Committee on the Education of Exceptional Children and Youth, composed of presidents and deans of higher institutions of learning. This committee developed a coordinated teacher training program offered at The University of Alabama, Auburn University, Tuskegee Institute, and Alabama A & M. Economically, at this time, it was not sound for all the colleges to offer this program as not enough people wanted it; also, trained personnel at the college level were scarce. The State Committee secured a grant of $50,000 from United Cerebral Palsy to provide an additional staff member at The University of Alabama and at Auburn University. Training in all areas was offered in our state except for the visually handicapped and the emotionally disturbed, and, before I left, training in the area of the emotionally disturbed was offered as well. Also, the University of South Alabama was approved for training of Special Education at the undergraduate and graduate level.

"The first college training in this field was offered by Dr. W. M. Anderson, assistant professor of Educational Psychology, 1952-56, at the University of Alabama, and by Dr. William Dorne at Auburn University. Other colleges offered work in Speech and Hearing. Dr. Jasper Harvey at the University of Alabama was the first full time professor of Special Education, beginning in 1959-60.

"We had classes and services available for all types of crippled children. These children had three types of services: Special classes, hospital teachers, and homebound instruction. There were classes for the deaf, hard-of-hearing, aphasoid, blind, partially-seeing, those with speech problems, educable mentally retarded, trainable mentally retarded, and other health problems. We had classes at the sanitorium in Flint and in Tuscaloosa and we had two groups which we called socially maladjusted classes, housed in the Juvenile Court in Birmingham.

"Regarding the growth of the program: in 1954-55 we had forty-eight physically handicapped classes; in 1955-56 we had 106 in many types of handicapping conditions, and we always had more requests for classes than we could honor. There were two years during which we only received ten new classes due to proration of funds, but in 1968 when I retired, we had 600 classes serving 10,000 children in 94 out of our 118 school systems in Alabama. I must recognize the help we received from agencies working with the handicapped, and also from the P.T.A., civic clubs, and the Rehabiliation and Crippled Children's Service.

"Now, going back . . . in 1957, I thought it was time we were a part of the A.E.A. In order to become a part, a group had to meet successfully for three years. I thought we could have forty at the first meeting, so I asked for a room that size. I had secured Dr. John Tenny from Detroit State University as speaker. The crowd kept coming, so we knew we had to have a larger place; luckily, we found one, and we had over one hundred to attend the meeting. We had published over one hundred copies of our first newsletter, and though I thought that would be far more then we would need, they were soon exhausted, and we still had requests for them. After three years, we became Branch 368 of the National Council for Exceptional Children and Youth; by 1962 we had over 100 members and were entitled to a representative on the National Board of Governors. I was the first Governor, serving a three-year term. On January 15, 1967 we became The Alabama Federation of Exceptional Children. There have to be at least two chapters in the State before a federation can be organized, and Mr. William Geer, executive director of National C.E.C., Washington, D.C., was quite impressed that we had eight chapters, the largest number in the nation at the beginning of a federation. A native of Alabama, he was very proud of our accomplishments in the state.

"In 1958, we wanted to host a Dupont Nemours Conference, especially since I had attended one in Georiga. At that time, money being scarce, I assured the Superintendent of Education it would not cost the State Department one cent to have the conference since the Nemours Foundation would pay all the expenses and also furnish consultants in all areas of disability. It was a three-day conference and doctors, nurses, psychologists, teachers, and agencies working with the handicapped had representatives there. Parents and other interested people attended, and besides the general assemblies, lunches, and banquets, there were small group discussions. The Junior League did the leg work and Mr. Bagley, Dr. Myers, and I formed the coordinating committee. This committee, with a representative from Junior League, met for several weeks of planning. A complete report was published following the conference which was attended by six hundred people. Dr. Shands, Executive Director of the Dupont Nemours Foundation, said it was the largest first-time crowd they had ever had. The following conferences were smaller because they dealt with only one handicapping condition. We held annual workshops for five years, and the Nemours Foundation made it possible for us to have two or three outstanding consultants in the areas being studied. All I had to do was to call Dr. Shands and tell him everything we wanted, and he never refused to send the amount of money we requested. After each conference, a report—giving in full the addresses of the consultants and the minutes of the group meetings—was published and sent to all Special Education teachers. After Federal Aid was available, the foundation set up other projects. *(It was my good fortune to participate in that first Nemours conference. D.S.)*

"Reba Penn King was the first consultant to help me. She came in 1963 and did excellent work with us for two and a half years. The second consultant was Gale Lambright, who left us to finish her doctorate; she too was excellent, and helpful in fighting some of our early battles. A number of others were added while I was there.

"The education of Exceptional Children and Youth is a team affair. The work of the doctors, nurses, psychologists, therapists, parents and teachers must parallel each other. Each must know what the others are doing if the best results are to be obtained. This program presents a challenge to all Alabamians."

Mrs. Alpha Brown was indeed a pioneering figure in Special Education in the state of Alabama and will long serve as an example of what can be accomplished when one has a driving purpose and boundless energy. At the time of Alpha's retirement, a number of tributes to her and her many accomplishments were published in the monthly newsleter of the Alabama Teachers of Exceptional Children. According to Mr. O. F. Wise, the Program for Exceptional Children and Youth, under Alpha's leadership, "has made tremendous strides and the educational opportunties that have been developed are recognized as being the best in the country." Mrs. Sarah Nesbitt added that, "Alpha Brown will be greatly missed. As this dedicated worker for the educational rights of handicapped children leaves us, she leaves behind a challenge and a heritage for her successors to emulate." According to Dr. Jasper Harvey, "Research seems to indicate that for Special Education to exist, there have to be trained teachers, adequate facilities, and an accepting school system. These Alpha Brown tried to provide for the exceptional children and youth of Alabama."

Following are the texts of my presentation speech at Mrs. Brown's retirement in 1969, a lovely letter which Alpha sent me in response to my presentation, and another letter from Alpha which I received at the time of my retirement.

Presentation Speech
At Mrs. Alpha Brown's Retirement in 1969

I'm not the oldest person around the state in CEC, I'm just the oldest one who would admit it! I'm not even the first president of the Teachers of Exceptional Children in Alabama. We should have had Mamie Shirley back from California or Sarah Nesbitt, our first president, to give you this little history of our state teachers organizaton and of the Council for Exceptional Children in Alabama. The program listed my part as historian of Special Education in the state. I have worried because so many of the fine, well-trained people in Special Education leave our state, but as I've grown older and wiser I realize there's no point in worrying about it. Now I recognize that it's the best ones who stay in Alabama!

We began as a state organization about twelve years ago, with such a little handful of people that it amazes some of us when we get together today. You can't go very far, in fact you can't even get started discussing any work touching on Exceptional Children without coming across the name of one person who—along with some fellow from Texas—spearheaded most of what has been done in this area; who led, pushed, pulled, dragged some of us in order to get things going! Today she calls herself "retired" but not a person in this room believes it. We know she's not that old; in fact, I know she's my age and I was already dreaming of inviting her to travel some with George, Ben, and me to South America and Switzerland when we both retired in a few years and here she's jumped the gun on me! It came as quite a shock to me expecially when I realized that it almost cost me my job. You haven't lived until you have answered the telephone on a hot July day and had one of your superior "superiors" (from the state department) say, "Do you know what a mess you've made of things?" Of course I said "No," (but actually with thirty interns I was beginning to feel that possibly I had). I just didn't think anyone else knew it.

So, I listened to an account of what I had done. I had invited this person to visit my two local Title VI School programs on Monday - the same day a surprise farewell luncheon had been planned for her. By the law of averages, she never should have accepted anyway, because she was certain to be too busy packing, but of course she had said, "I'll be there by 7:00." So I did what any good, honest, law-abiding citizen would have done under the same circumstances - told a little white lie! I called back, and have always been so thankful that she wasn't in and that I could leave a message with the secretary, saying the the two supervisors felt it was too near the end of the summer term for visitors!

Since you call yourself "retired", let me pass on a few gems about growing old gracefully. These are from internship notes of modern times so a few of you will have to excuse this. Dr. Harvey thought we had doubled the credit hours in order to give the students more practical experiences; it's really so I can get in all these little poems and stories!

> *"A man is not old when his hair has turned gray,*
> *A man is not old when his teeth decay,*
> *But he's well on his way to that long, long sleep,*
> *When his mind makes appointments that his body can't keep."*

OR

"A sure sign of advancing age is when you wake up feeling like the morning after the night before and you didn't do anything the night before."

OR

*I've learned to live with bi-focals,
my dentures fit me fine,
I'm making it with my arthritis,
but, oh how I miss my mind."*

And surely this explains Alpha's leaving us: "My dear old dad remarked long ago, if your hopes and dreams fade a bit, if things don't go quite right, my girl, stand up like a man - and quit!" Mrs. Alpha Brown, will you come up here?

As long as there is an exceptional child in Alabama, as long as there's a teacher or parent or Department of Education trying to do what is needed for one child, as long as there's a school superintendent pondering over the problems of a special education program or the director of an institution trying to meet the needs of his or as long as there are colleges and universities trying to meet the demands of training additional workers for the field, your influence will be felt. There is no one is this room who has failed to be inspired by your devotion to your task, your boundless enthusiasm and energies as you literally built the program from nothing as our first Chief Consultant, Exceptional Children and Youth. We will continue to profit by all you preached and practiced. Come to see us anytime and don't fail to advise us when we need it. On behalf of the Alabama Federation of the Council for Exceptional Children, it is one of the greatest pleasures of my life to have the honor of presenting to you this silver tray as a token of our high esteem and love for you.

Daisy Styles

Dear Daisy:

Well, you did a beautiful job in making the presentation of my gift. However, I will say you were most generous in your praise. One never feels they deserve such gifts for, after all, I was just doing my job the best I knew how. Of course I'm flattered and appreciate all the nice things that were done. I also appreciate the biannual Alpha Brown Service Award and the standing ovation. I never had had that before!

Also, a thing I thought of a great deal was the fact that the two main secretaries who had worked for me for five years came to Birmingham to see me because they didn't know I was going to Montgomery. They are fine secretaries and my good friends.

I enjoyed my visit to the State Department of Education. I tried to see everyone with whom I have worked closely. I'd planned on one hour; it took three hours. Time flies when you just spend a few minutes with everyone. Most of them were curious about how I accepted retirement. No one need ever worry about time hanging on their hands. I don't have time to do all the things I want to do. The advantage is you can do things at your pleasure and do what you want to do.

Your seminar was excellent. I thought that you had capable people attending and they all had an interest in Special Education. Everything I saw and heard indicated to me that Special Education in Alabama is on the move in the right direction.

Again, thanks for a very enjoyable visit and you have an invitation to visit me at your convenience. Just let me know.

Do write when you can.

Sincerely,
Alpha

6115 West Markham, Apt. 1-L
Little Rock, Arkansas 72205
February 1, 1976

Dear Daisy,

It has been a pleasure to know and work with you a number of years. I must thank you for all the help and work you have done for Special Education. In the early days only those of us who were in it realize all the problems we had.

Your leadership was such a help to the Program. Your classroom was a place we could send teachers and others to see some techniques necessary to have a good class.

Developing an understanding of the Program by professionals and the general public was important and you made a big contribution there. We always depended on you at conferences, new projects and various organizational work. Your work at the University of Alabama presented the Program in such a practical, convincing way that your students came through with an understanding of the work involved. I'm sure you will always be a help to Special Education.

Best wishes for your retirement.

Love,
Alpha

Chapter Five
THE CARE AND NURTURING

"All the flowers of all the tomorrows are in the seeds of today".

—from a sampler in Aunt Pearl's kitchen.

The Buds
From Classes at Verner and Cottondale Schools:

Tuscaloosa County established two special classes for the educable mentally retarded in January, 1956, one at Northport Elementary and one at Cottondale, with Charles Sprayberry and George Styles serving as principals. Tuscaloosa City Schools had established its first classes at Northington School with Mrs. Clara McRimmon as principal. Mrs. Hardy Perritt was the first teacher at Cottondale, with Mrs. Eugene Branscomb at Northport, and Mrs. Mildred Olson at Northington.

The class at Cottondale with fifteen pupils was housed in the principal's small office, but this wasn't as bad as it seems because the sixth grade was being taught by the principal in the outer reception office and the fifth grade in the hall. A new school had been built in 1955 to care for about 300 pupils; enrollment at the old school had been 150. The next fall, over 500 pupils showed up, and plans for building a new wing (or at least the first four rooms of a new wing) were made immediately.

So it was that I became the teacher of the special class, still held in George's office, in September 1957. By now there were 17 pupils, ages 7 to 16, but it didn't seem too bad. There was an outside door, full use of the teacher's rest room, a hall outside the room, and even folding cots for use after lunch each day. At the same time there was the opportunity to help plan the new special class room. It was to be complete with a bath room and hot shower, though these were the only added features beyond what all other classrooms had.

The day came for furniture to be ordered. The superintendent, Dr. Kermit Alonzo Johnson, or the principal, or perhaps both, suggested that, since the special class would only need fifteen to twenty units, they could possibly just use the best of the old furniture, but when the order came, the special class had new furniture, too. I had not thrown any fits, but I said firmly, "Tell me one reason why these children don't deserve new furniture just as much as any others in this school."

A day in 1960 stands out so vividly, the day that two brothers had their first showers. These boys had not even had nearly enough "spit" baths, and I could understand why after making a home visit. They had a loving set of parents, but that was about it, except for the bare necessities of life—two beds, a wood stove, a few chairs and a table—and there was no bathroom. Situations like this made a difference in my teaching, because you don't dwell on waxing floors, straightening closets, polishing furniture, running the washer, or baking fruit cake. Instead, you talk about sweeping down cobwebs, picking up garbage, and washing clothes in a tub outside the house.

But, back to the bath. Memory fails as to which child went first. Little academic teaching went on for an hour, and through the walls of that tile bath could be heard laughter; the teacher laughed too, not at the kids but with them. By the time the second shower came on, the water was running completely out under the bathroom door into the classroom. We took turns mopping it up and continued to laugh. That was one of my happiest days in any class during all of the thirty years of my career, and there was genuine pride the part of that entire group. After baths, the boys washed their clothes in a pan at the sink, and hung them on hangers from the limb of our gum tree right outside the windows. They combed their hair, and the trade school barber class, in what became a regular occurrence, gave them free haircuts with Mrs. Jimmy Swain being one of our regular PTA drivers, taking boys from other classes also. All of the class then begged to take showers at school; most who had tubs probably didn't have showers at home. The problem of some going home stating that "Mrs. Styles let (or made) me take a bath today", knowing that some might not understand why, was solved by saying,

"You bring a note from home and your own towel (since we don't use each other's towels) and that will be fine." You can guess that, for awhile, showers took part of each day. Some were afraid of the shower, so I gave them lessons on the safe use of hot water, and they learned to clean bathrooms. Never again did we have any reason for being ashamed if visitors came in, and the whole school, even that first day noted the difference in some of the students. Of course we let the entire faculty know that if a child had a bathroom accident, they should feel free to use our shower. After my happy days at Cottondale, it was a sad day to find that the special class, taught by Barbara Jackson, had moved out of that nice room into a portable.

Every classroom at Cottondale had a very valuable outside door. A very disturbed little boy who came to me from the first grade, could sit in front of that open door when he couldn't stand the entire group another minute without screaming or hitting somebody. He would rock in my own first-generation children's rocking chair, play soft music on the record player, or look at a book or at the beauty of nature outside. I always had to be the partner of Wayman, another memorable student. The first time we started to "dance", he literally got down on his hands and knees and begged not to have to dance with a girl partner. "Whip me, anything, but don't make me ask a girl to dance!" I asked if I would be acceptable and I was. By the time the record said "change partners" the ice had been broken and I suspect he went on to high school and changed his mind about girls! Roger Ballard's sixth grade would invite us to come dance with them, and we never refused. What fun we had square-dancing! How patient with us they were on "Alemande left" and "Do si do" if we got mixed up.

Our first Christmas we made whipped parafin candles as gifts for parents, other teachers, lunchroom workers, supervisors, the superintendent, friends, and especially enemies, meaning those who didn't believe in Special Education. We read directions and learned safety and those children figured out better ways to make the candles than any of the directions we found in books though in "Singing Wheels" we found a story about how the early settlers used to dip candles, and we read it with glee. By the next Christmas, people pleaded to have us make gift candles to sell in our school store. We did, and even took orders. You'd think that's all we did all day, but all of our usual teaching went on. In the fall, using yarn, we made black and red and purple and white pom-poms, tied with ribbon, and they were worn on lapels to the Tuscloosa Black Bear and Holt Ironmen football games. We sold them for 50 cents each, much cheaper than a corsage, and even our trainables could do a good job making them. When we made plaster-molded bust figures of Lincoln and Washington in February, we learned to just paint the entire thing with black tempera paint and then wash it at the sink under a stream of water. This gave a beautiful effect and our athetoid cerebral palsied one could do this well. This could even be done with multi-colored objects.

Did all the children fight to be first? How did we decide who would carry on the first step process while everybody else was still reading, writing, or doing arithmetic? After a group lesson, and with some individual or small group assignments made, the best process I discovered was to have them write their name by a number in order on the board after a certain assignment was satisfactorily completed. They all knew their turn would come so there was no racing to be first and a poorly done assignment could require re-doing! From this I learned to always have a system for everything done in a special class. If you don't think that's motivation, try it. When you say, "Your arithmetic will be finished first," be sure you mean it. Many of these youngsters haven't found much they can depend on in life, so the teacher should be sure that she doesn't add to it. This brings me back to that thing of meaning what you say. The day comes to mind, a Monday, when Colin (regular class before 1957) balked at completing an arithmetic assignment. It was one the teacher knew he could do! Play period was the only thing he liked about school. (I really don't like to, or seldom did take away play periods with "special" children. They need it too badly. So does the teacher.) Nothing else worked with him and many things had been tried. There were several teachers on the playground so it was possible for one to stay in her room occasionally. So I did resort to "We'll stay till you finish your math. It won't take long." He balked, scowled, didn't pick up his pencil the entire time. I graded papers, went on about my business, and seemed not to notice he wasn't doing it. Next day, same thing! This went on till about Thursday. Finally when he realized he wasn't getting anywhere, and football season would soon end, he picked up his pencil, grinned at me, I at him, he completed it - and we both went out to play. Never did we have the problem again and we finished school still friends. In fact, he came to see us after he went away to the Navy. He wrote the only apologetic letter after he went away to the Navy that George ever got in his 36 years' teaching! How do you sell special education? Satisfied customers, the ads all say. And do you satisfy by being too easy, not requiring much? Not on your life. They can read you like a book.

We rested on folding cots every day, just after lunch. The days were long, especially for those who came first and left last. I have observed many special class teachers end rest period before it ever gets started, or give up on even trying to have one. It took about fifteen minutes for most of them to really settle down, especially the hyperactive ones, and there was turning and twisting before final relaxation. Maybe it just took longer in my class because of the teacher. With my kids it worked better if they didn't take a book or toy to bed with them, nor did I read to them while they rested. Even playing records or tapes seemed ineffective. When that restless time had passed, there was peace like I have not seen before or since, and I didn't have to take a university course later to learn that some types of cerebral-palsied people stop all jerking motions while asleep. I had a cot, and quite often I went to sleep too. Never once did I find a child up when I awoke, though some would be awake. My getting up was the signal and, one by one, they quietly put their cots on the stack. Mine was rotated so that I never had a "special" pet beside me nor did they again have to argue about whose cot would be by the teacher. This was the time of the day when individual work was done, or a little extra attention given to one who needed it, and no group lessons were planned for about an hour after rest. Sometimes, if one or two kids were awake, they and the teacher would sit under the gum tree and "share" on whatever subject seemed timely. Play period followed nap time, but we still didn't wake up the one still sleeping, unless he had asked us to before he went to sleep. I can recall one or two coming out almost daily at odd times during play period, but I don't recall anything ever being stolen while he was the last one left in the room. We had transom upper windows opening to the hall and one day I heard a child say to his teacher, "Why can't we have a rest period like the special class does?" The reply: "Your parents didn't send you to school to sleep. Get your spelling books out!" I would have liked to tell her how much better all the work might have been done following a brief rest period, but I didn't.

The next period was group time. Just as at rest time, it seemed to take a little while to really unwind after play. After drinks of water and trips to the rest room, this time was used to read them a story. In fact, we gathered for this as they came in, some sitting on the floor and some in chairs. As one went to the bathroom, others had an opportunity to share with the group and tapped the next person to go until all had been. One of the other discipline-reducing tricks I learned was to not force special class children to wait in long lines any more than necessary. As each child returned from washing hands before going to lunch, the next one went, taking his place in the large "circle" of chairs so that when it was time to go, everybody was ready and just returned his book to the ledge or library table, leaving the room in order and ready to come back to a restful atmosphere.

The day stands out when a ten-year old, emotionally disturbed child, kicked a first grade teacher. There was no other place for him so he became one of mine, and he did qualify as to IQ level. It was toward the end of school, and we felt he might be able to go back into a regular class in the fall at about third or fourth grade level, so we decided to let him take an achievement test with a third grade group. The teacher giving the test took them all to the drinking fountain at a break and had them stand in line. A very tired, pale child, who probably came to school without breakfast, the boy got weary of standing, so he leaned back with one foot raised and against the wall. It would leave a shoe mark, of course, and it was a pretty, clean, new school. When the teacher asked him to stand up straight in the line, he kicked her in the shin as he did what she said— before he took time to think—and began crying. She took him to the principal's office before he got hysterical. George brought him to me, told me a little of what had happened, and we saw there was no point in even trying to talk with him then, so I told George to let me wait awhile and see what I could do. Of course it was totally out of the question to even suggest he finish his test. Again, not keeping him in at play period as punishment, but just so we could talk privately, we stayed. He didn't want to go out anyway, apparently, because he had not raised his head from the desk top since returning. He was so ashamed of himself! I then heard a story that I wish I had on tape. He was sorry for what he did. He said, "Mrs. Styles, I am so tired! My Mama and Daddy had a party at the house last night. They all got drunk, and made so much fuss I didn't get any sleep. They do this all the time. I wish I could go somewhere else - anywhere else to live. Get them to send me to reform school, an orphan's home, or something!" It reminded me again what I had been taught in Child Psychology: that all behavior is caused and no child wants to be bad. I told George all of this. The teacher's husband and a very good friend was the school systems' Guidance Counselor. He came to school the next day and sincerely felt that the boy was a menace in a public school setting, that he was gaining nothing, and that he should be expelled. I pleaded that this not happen, not yet. I believe we did work out counseling for him, and I promised to do all I could. He was something of a problem but never that much of one. From that day on we had quite a rapport. It seemed to help so much to have told someone his problems, and he apologized to the teacher and tried hard to control himself. As I recall, he did amazingly well. Never again did I put him in any stressful situation if I could help it, and I was very conscious of this with all exceptional children from then on.

Don't underestimate the interest level of your classes. This is not to say one should teach above their heads, but if something you have tried to teach falls flat, change the subject. Don't let your classes be bored; life is too short for that. Of course, a certain amount of that is expected at the college level.

Among all those University students over a thirteen year period, at one time or another I tried nearly every method of teaching, and amazingly, most of them achieved their purpose with some success. The conclusion was reached that, "who is to say what method, processes, procedures are the ones to use in teaching a retarded, regular, or gifted class?" There were times, upon reading a unit in advance, that the first thought crossing my mind was: "That won't work!"

An example was the unit on architecture, presented to the Primary EMR group at Verner by the University architect, Mr. James Hankins. We were all spellbound, and they asked questions for much longer than their interest spans were supposed to last. He said no group had ever been as interested before, and he answered those questions in terms that even I could understand. The background for that unit was that it was the summer of the construction of Tutwiler Hall, right outside our windows. You surely couldn't close those windows in July heat with no air conditioning. Consequently, much of the summer was spent standing, watching the interesting procedures going on, all the equipment being used, and seeing a tremendous undertaking grow day by day. Oh, we did sit at our desks and do some reading, writing, and arithmetic. I've often felt sorry for children through the years when it snowed, and the teacher wouldn't let them stand for a while and watch the beauty of it.

A Little Boy and His Goats

This is another of those creative writings that I fully meant to preserve on tape or in written form. I have probably waited too long, because I have no idea where the author is. Bobby was one of those boys who could wrap his fingers around your heartstrings. He came from a broken home, with a father who had become an alcholic and a mother in Bryce Hospital, and the only sibling I can recall was a younger sister. They lived with their grandparents, who were caretakers at Camp Cherry Austin, the Girl Scout camp. One day, in "sharing time," Bobby held us spellbound with his story of the birth of two baby goats the night before, the coldest night of that winter. We never needed any lessons along this line again because a more beautiful story of the birth process was never heard. With all the tenderness and love possible, he persuaded his grandfather to let him bring the mother inside and I would guess the old gentlemen decided it might come to a choice between having a goat inside or a grandson freeze. Even inside, the babies would begin to freeze to the delivery table as soon as they came, and it took some real problem solving to avoid this. Grandpa went on to bed but Bobby stayed up all night to see that the incubator stayed warm, and gave the mother—who was his own pet—all the care that any obstetrician could have. Wouldn't he have made a good veterinatian's helper? Instead, the last time I saw him, he was floundering, not living up to promises, unemployed, and trying to help that younger sister. They missed their grandparents after they were gone. Everybody needs somebody.

This story recalls the many animals which played a part in the activities for my special classes. There were the earthworm eggs brought so carefully from a farm but never hatched. The child involved had his self-concept greatly improved by all the attention this brought him and he needed it so badly; also a lot of science was studied by my pupils because of it. The children had a great big garden then at school and knew that earthworms serve a real purpose in cultivation of the soil. We meant to sell the radishes, onions, and cabbage to the school lunchroom, but most of it was taken home to be proudly consumed. It was a year when the season was not right so that everything was late, and children paraded back to school in June to harvest the rest of the cabbage. We did this once even during summer school, about five miles from the University. About every other day, the red University van could be seen with Jerry Aldridge driving going out in the afternoon when school was over for the day (or was it Joe Powell?).

Then there was the mother crayfish, brought by the twins George and Gerald, with a tremendous sac of eggs on her stomach, or back. Each Friday I lugged the fish bowl home so that, if they hatched, proper incubation could be achieved. They hatched on a Sunday, millions of them, and on Monday the children watched all those little, red, crawly things, still nesting on the mother's back, until it was time to either get rid of them or the thirty-nine first graders. They were returned to their natural habitat.

On the walk to Barnwell Hall each day during summer school, I never knew what my purse might hold before the day ended. Sometimes there would be a purse full of big red and black grasshoppers, or a pretty yellow and black butterfly. We kept the snakes scared away, but one of my grandsons compensated for that by always having one in a shoe box next door. He came to Verner one day and showed us his iguana and told us all about it. We once conducted an animal experiment with the diets of white mice, given to us free from the University Nutrition Department. One rat was not fed milk, and he did not grow at all, while the other rat thrived and had a glossy white coat of fur. The children named the milkless one Charles because one pupil by that name didn't drink milk either. They could hardly wait to get the experiment over with and "fatten" Charles up, and they really did!

The pets my pupils couldn't bring to school were discussed at length during "sharing" time each morning. We once had a conference and decided that we were going to let a boy named Perry have all the time he wanted just once. The leader handed out work sheets, took them up, distributed books and colors, and Perry was still talking at lunchtime. Anybody passing would have thought it was a Congressional filibuster.

Mrs. Abbie Lawrence West, who retired from Vance School, did my substitute teaching, and she taught me and my pupils so much. Once, on my first day back, there was George Albert's name in big letters on the board. The thought, "What did he do?" went through my mind. Later, when his bus arrived, he could hardly wait to tell me what he had done. "She said I was the best rester in the class." Forever after that he was. Find something complimentary to say to each of your pupils everyday. Mrs. Bessie Booth, who always spoke at my final student teaching seminar, stressed this.

One assembly program composed of a series of stories concerning things that had taken place in special class. The pupils decided what would be included, planned the program, and wrote their own speeches. George Albert wanted to tell about how we all watched a little squirrel do a tight-rope act across a power line from one wing of the building to another. The morning of the program, he got cold feet and said he couldn't do it, but on the stage, he gave a signal not to omit his part. All the pupils held their breath as he went to the mike. George, who seldom wanted to speak publicly, gave a Gettsyburg address about the little squirrel who almost fell but made it, with everybody rooting for him. We were so proud of him, and he of himself.

Roy, another special pupil, went to the office with a message for the principal. He sent one back instead, "What in the name of the world is it you want?" He could not communicate very well, but he declared that what he asked for was Hakahaw. He wanted Alcohol.

One day Verner grounds were very wet and muddy from a rain the night before, but with a hyperactive bunch—especially the interns—you don't let that stop you. A girl named Anne always was the last one in after recess so somebody usually kept an eye on her as the rest of us marched in. This time when she came lumbering in the back door she was not wearing one stitch of clothes. Anne had taken a last turn down the slide, splashing right into a mud puddle, and she could make a big splash. Who wants to wear wet, muddy clothes and mess up a nice clean room? How's that for problem solving?

One of the characteristics of a child, especially one in our classes, is their complete honesty, though I thought they outgrew it in adulthood. Johnny, with an IQ of 49, came to see us after he was grown to show us his new car, to tell us about his good job at a sawmill, and to let us meet his future wife, in that order of importance. His greeting was, "Mr. Styles, you haven't changed a bit, but Mrs. Styles surely has gotten older and fatter." I knew I should have failed him years before!

My pupils taught me a great deal. One day I was desperately trying to get a screw out of something with a screw driver, and I kept hoping it might accidentally come out. A boy named Richard said, "You need a Phillips head screw driver," and showed me the difference.

The Blossoms.
Daisy's Darlings
My University of Alabama Classes

"I use not only the brains I have but all I can borrow."
—Woodrow Wilson

Each semester from 1962-1975 we summarized our work, trying especially to recall the funny things, and things that could still teach us lessons. One of the intern graduate students, (undergraduates we called student teachers) came up with the name above. Was it Wanda Walton? The following are a few excerpts.

Summer, 1966
The Other Side of Internship

Theme for the Summer: "I know you believe you understand what you think I said, but I am not sure you realize that what you heard is not what I meant." Copied from the walls of Smith-Woods.

News soon leaked out that the major motivating factor for so many students enrolling for the course was the false rumor that we travel all the time. Where could such an idea have come from? And who could forget Mrs. Niles giving assignments to her people for the 4th of July! She just accidentally stumbled on the news of a holiday because her husband also worked for the University.

Imagine starting, and ending, a course and not having a U. of A. classroom and not being sure from one day to the next which building you are supposed to go to for seminars. This uncertainty probably boosted attendance, however, since a student didn't dare miss the announcement about where to meet the next day. Also this meant that no one dared not come to Verner daily, and sometimes twice daily, to be sure the room number hadn't changed.

Imagine having 3 people in the pool who, by their own admission, couldn't swim! Miss Hanna Gillion didn't know this. Thirteen wet heads went to a class called Psychology of The Mentally Retarded each day, and they never did figure out the best procedure for all this early morning dressing. What was one to do with a wet suit all day? The options were: (1) Wear suit to school, bring good clothes in a suit case. (2) Dress to come to school, bring bathing suit in purse. (3) Just wear wet suit all day with a shift over it. (4) Just wear wet suit.

A few ulterior motives just may have entered in for so many volunteers to help with swimming:

A-The fact that an announcement was made that you don't even have to bring a suit to swim. U of A provided them to present a daily Miss America contest!

B-That they Barnwell jerseys, when wet, develop necklines that sag to the knees!

C-That you can't afford lunch anyway and need to lose weight.

D-That you someday may be a student teacher in SPE and,

have this same old set-in-her-ways instructor to try to supervise it so maybe a few bonus points in advance won't hurt! Just wait till the first one says, "You remember me? I have already put in my 500 hours for no credit, so I won't need to attend any seminars; all I want is my A.

Wilson Dietrich added a new theme to his parent-counseling session early in the term: "Be careful what you say to staff members. They are a sensitive lot." A mother at Hackberry House, when introduced to a certain mother-daughter team, indicated that it's hard to know which is the daughter! But that's all right, because later in the term, when another mother stated that she also had two exceptional children, the staff member made a rare(?) slip of the tongue and retaliated with, "How nice!" Was it the undertaker's idea of, "That's how I happen to be in business?" No, really, it was just that when a mother starts talking about her children, one tunes her out, and when she is through says, "How nice!"

This semester will always be remembered for the following incidents, among others: Hearing a six-year-old speak in the pre-school who hadn't done much of it before. Seeing the look in a daddy's eyes as he shows you the picture of his new daughter and says, "She can really kick those legs!" His first child was born a year and a half before with spina bifida, and was paralyzed from the waist down. Renting a trailer to a former EMR student, and helping him to get a job with a dandy understanding boss; seeing his struggle to make it when he never had the security of a mother and daddy. Seeing student teachers eager to learn all they can that will help them next year, and going far beyond the minimal requirements of the course. Seeing 100 exceptional children experience the fun of swimming, having volunteer helpers handle this almost entirely, and hearing teachers say what a difference it has made in so many problems.

Who could forget hearing an outstanding Negro educator tell us some of the "lacks" in the lives of black children which are complicating their problems, and of some of the confusing "undercurrents" facing young blacks and whites. I heard a retired teacher tell young teachers of the jobs which lie ahead of them, of some ways to face some of their problems, and of their powerful influence on young people. I heard M. L. Roberts, Assistant Dean of the College of Education, say to my student teaching seminar, "The day has come when the teacher shortage is over. We must do some weeding out! People still have a right to expect more from teachers than from other people so let us watch the attitudes of our young, prospective teachers, and if they are unwilling to shape up and fit in with standards imposed by their teaching situations, then let's let them ship out." A great deal of spontaneous applause followed this and there were many young people in the audience.

Fall, 1972

Another semester gone—and again I've heard myself saying, "This is the best group ever!" And they were very exceptional—especially in one way. They were all female—not even the usual lone wolf among them. But we did have one cooperating teacher of the opposite sex—Luther Gibson.

It was again a semester of some other firsts: My first experience with a doctoral student to assist in supervision of the 17 student teachers. Who can ever forget Hilde (no one who ever meets her!)? Especially her Piaella! And especially Stanley Goldstein, Connie Nichols, the Andalusia School System, and the Foreign Car Center!

Bernice, a little midget, isn't exactly a first but actually a second, because she survived summer school, as my and Loretta's personal secretary, swimming and all, with 49 student teachers and interns! She couldn't believe all those evaluation forms she typed would ever be used up, but they were! And when time came to plan for the Spring semester, the 100 packets for schools were depleted so fast that she didn't even get through with Loretta's typing before she had to start preparing another 100! We'd never have made it without her!

Then there was a first we'll never forget! The blessing asked by James in my special class so many years ago came to mind that day, "Lord forgive us for what we are about to receive!"

We finally (in our spare moments) all got our heads together and came up with some common expectations for all our programs for future student teachers—Jim, Loretta, and Linda have been so nice to work with. We may never follow them, and may ditch the whole thing next year, but it was worth something just to come up with them. We even rewrote our evaluation forms—in behavorial objectives!   Sixty-five people passed the test of a covered dish dinner at Loretta's house on a hot December night with the air-——conditioner going. She hasn't figured yet how she's going to explain that to her Arkansas friends!

Another first—our third annual, nice, jolly, friendly, handsome, married, father of three, capable head of the undergraduate program—Dr. Bob Palk! We all feel that we've finally found one nice enough to stay awhile! (We lost Charlie Horn to the Paty Hall project and Marion Thompson moved on.) Incidentally, looks as though this one may really be a first—each of our other two had a baby before the year was out—and here it is midterm.

Another first—imagine two new women faculty members! They finally decided women aren't so bad after all. And all in the same office, as well as a secretary, and a doctoral assisant (also women) Talk about segregation! Wards at the hospital couldn't be more so. But at least we have a glass partition looking into the men's ward!

A final first—it will also be remembered as the semester we lost both secretaries—and neither had survived a year. What kinds of men do we have over there?   One wonders if the question overheard across the way frightened them away. Two male faculty members were doing some future planning and one said, "Now just what is it we're planning to do during our intercourse? (Takes awhile for people to learn Alabama language and the phrase "interim" course is what he meant to say!).

That I should quit on!

Chapter Six

THE FUN OF HARVESTING

"Laughter is God's hand on the shoulders of a troubled world."

—Author unknown

Maybe you have already gotten the impression that teaching was fun. It was. Some of these recollections seem to have real importance today.

Amazing Grace

On the walls of Forest Manor Nursing Home, May 18, 1985, I read the following anecdote. Mrs. Grace Hamby was Shirley's and George's math teacher at Alberta Junior High School and truly was amazing.

"She taught for 47 years before her retirement in 1966. Her first teaching certificate was issued when she was sixteen. She received a salary of $50.00 per month. During World War II she left teaching to be a secretary in a defense office, war bond office, then to become secretary to the president of the University of Alabama. Finally, she returned to her first love of teaching.

As she was grading a test one day she read at the bottom what a student had written: 'The Lord loveth a cheerful giver.'

Below that Mrs. Hamby wrote, 'The Lord helps those who help themselves.'"

Speech Problems of Exceptional Children had a reputation for being one of the more difficult courses, what with all of the technical names of parts of the speech mechanism, all five sinuses, etc. Adapted Physical Education ran it a close second with all the names of muscles, tendons, and ligaments, but Dr. Harvey didn't teach that one. Those were my first and last courses for credit. On the day prior to the final in Speech Problems, the entire class panicked. Even in class, they sat with their noses to the grindstone, trying to cram it all in. Dr. Harvey stood it as long as he could and said, "If you folks will just listen to my final lecture, and quit being so nervous, I'll cancel the exam." You can bet they happily complied with that request.

In Louise Temerson's class in Adapted Physical Education, I was the only non-physical education member, and was 44 years old, twice the age of most students. Word did, even then, get around as to what would be included on the exam, so I crammed all night trying to learn about things like flexors. In SPE courses the terminology had been simple, with terms like encephalography, pneumoencephalogram, indogenous, exogenous, prognosis, psychomotor, Gargolysm, etilogy, hydrocephalic, somaesthetic. To my amazement, this very human teacher totally deleted all those technical parts of the exams with which she thought I might have trouble. I started to write down all I knew just so she would know I had studied. This was very different from the question Dr. Harvey asked on an exam. I had never heard of it before! I just answered it by saying what I had read somewhere, "It is better to keep silent and be thought a fool than to speak and remove all doubt". I did want Mrs. Temerson to know that SPE majors can memorize as well as PE majors. I have wondered if, forever after, PE majors have tried to bribe some elderly SPE major to enroll in that course each semester.

There was a time when money permitted us to make field trips, and it was such a valuable experience because so many delightful programs existed, all so different. With one of our first and largest groups, we were leaving early to visit centers in Mobile. My last step in grooming, just before the scheduled departure time to meet students at Verner, was to brush my hair. As soon as I had made the first few strokes I realized something was drastically wrong. A look in the mirror revealed hair that was oiled and pasted down to my scalp, and nothing would lift it; there was nothing I could do because it would have taken an hour and ten applications of shampoo to half-way unglue it. My little two-year old granddaughter, visiting from next door the night before, had generously massaged herself with baby oil and used my hair brush to rub it in. She had likely read my notes on the importance of developing a kinesthetic sense. Dr. Harvey, always immaculately dressed and groomed, was waiting at Verner to see that we got off on time and when he saw me, he turned pale and then every shade of the rainbow. He tried to speak and so did I, but we were both speechless. George always said that if you have to explain it, don't. That was the last time the Department Chairman ever saw any of my groups off, remembering how terrible I looked as I left to go all over the state representing that great university. He probably told people that I was from Auburn, our archrival institution for which we do have great respect!

Field tripping was always fun and very educational. Sometimes it was with thirty students, sometimes with three. There was a time we went to Dothan to visit Anne Ramsey's class, among others. She had taught English to my son George in the ninth grade before entering SPE. He said she was the best young teacher he ever had. Was he indicating that age and experience can bring some expertise? This trip was one of those with just three students in the old Chevelle, when a University car was not available. It wasn't always easy to get one at 4:00 or 5:00 a.m. We tried not to be too costly and made one-day runs as much as possible, many times putting in a full work day of eight hours just driving, plus six to eight hours visiting. This day, John Paul Biancuzzo assisted with the driving, but I felt I had best do the inner-city driving. After all, he had faced New York City driving many times but this may not have given him enough experience. On the return trip, just at the edge of town, a siren broke the silence. The patrolman said, "Lady, do you know you are breaking the speed limit in a school zone?" I tried to explain that I did slow down to 20 MPH but thought we were out of the zone. He was very kind because of the out-of-town tag, or maybe the U of A sticker. John Paul drove the rest of the way home, and this experience made us lasting friends. He is one who keeps in touch, wrote to me of his wedding, and about his jobs. Dr. Harvey almost fainted when he learned later that his uncle was a congressman, very instrumental in passing laws relating to federal grants, and that we might have turned John Paul down for a fellowship without knowing.

We almost lost one of our husbands (we were not polygamists) on one of our field trips to a Rehabilitation Center. George (not mine) was quadraplegic so Kay drove her car so that he could go along. He had the use of one finger, so he made his living typing term papers while lying in bed. At the end of our tour, one the therapists started to cart him away in his wheel chair. He was yelling, "I'm one of them." but it took all of our group to convince them that a client was not trying to escape.

When a group of student teachers made a field trip to visit centers in Chattanooga, I took Ben along because he was left at home so often, though his daddy did a better job with him than I did, but this was a busy time for George. We visited the Orange Grove pre-school center. Norman Bissell was the director there and I am sure he has not forgotten how he tried to persuade me to leave Ben in a class his age while we made our rounds. He finally succeeded, and upon my return, Ben was sound asleep on a cot as were all the others. They then enjoyed cookies and milk while I observed through the two-way mirror, amazed that he had not even missed me. That night, just at bedtime, he looked at his hand and asked, "When can I get a fork on my hand?" The child beside him had no fingers but in their place was a prosthetic device. I don't even remember how I answered him. You can just never tell the effects of special education!

There was another field trip to schools and centers in the Mobile area when a certain graduate student found one of her most embarrassing moments. The group was traveling in her station wagon and stopped for a restroom break. When the respected instructor came out of the rest room, she was horrified to see her students driving off without her. Quite a chase ensued. A red-faced Cam Pennington Saunders backed up and met her halfway. Surely a teacher is missed more than that.

My family was at home at night, and I tried to be also. I always told my married students that it was a real trick to make your husband and family and, at the same time, your boss feel that they were each the most important part of your life. Jasper Harvey often reminded me that he expected my family to come first.

One day George Jr. invited me to meet him and his Gulf States cronies at Catfish Cabin for lunch. I did and as I sat there with 8 or 10 young men, in came my entire college of education faculty! They all stared because they knew I never had but one male student teacher in each class, so I felt compelled to introduce them. I still don't think most of them knew I had a son except the three-year-old one.

From Lila Niles White: "I have known George and Daisy for many years and George and I have limited our affection to a kiss at the airport in Birmingham. Daisy and thirty-five other Special Education teachers were there at the time as we all left for the Council for Exceptional Children Convention in Dallas, Texas in 1973.

"My stepson Bill is principal at Buhl Elementary School. He had been ill with the flu but insisted on going back to work. One morning I decided to call and check on him. I dialed the number and asked the secretary for Mr. Niles. She replied, 'Just a minute.' A voice then said, 'Hello' and I replied 'How are you this morning, honey?' The voice replied, 'What a nice way to start the day!' I realized that, instead of dialing Buhl, I had looked at the number below in the school directory and was talking to George Styles. Needless to say, I was quite embarrassed, but George recovered nicely when I tried to explain my circumstances." How I did have to watch these co-workers, especially those who had once been students!

Shirley, during high school days, did some volunteer work at Partlow State School, helping with recreational activities, and she once came home from a dance saying, "You know I have a hard time telling who are the residents and who are the workers!

You may be wondering about the shady deal that got my family member on the University Staff at Hackberry. That first summer session was preceded by daily queries from Gale Lambright and Jasper wondering where in the world they were going to find a qualified housemother for the residential program with children who were physically handicapped. I listened to their requirements:

1. Someone who can be gone from home and family all summer
2. A good motherly type used to losing sleep over sick children
3. Someone with a knowledge of quantity cooking
4. Someone who is well and strong
5. A person who can work for minimum wage or less

(it was an expensive program and not much money was left from federal grants).

It dawned on me that they were describing my mother exactly but I still waited a few days to let my womanly intuition tell me for sure. Besides, they were about to get so desperate that I was afraid they might soon ask me to be housemother after I finished teaching at Verner everyday. At lunch one day I broached the subject to Gale and Jasper. So help me, he wanted my mother's telephone number right then, but I told him she would still be at her job as lunchroom manager of Craig Air Force Base School. He waited till 4:00. She immediately said, "Why sure. I'd love to come!" She jumps to conclusions, too, and wants things done right now. She would do anything to get out of babysitting with Ben, and doing all of my cooking, laundry, and housework, which she had already done the last two summers. It dawned on me too late what a horrible thing I had done.

Daddy had died in 1960, leaving her with one child in college, and an empty nest. She drew Social Security in the summers so could only receive a small salary. What a time she had! I believe it was the most memorable event of her entire life, as you can tell from the following letter. She had only had cancer, heart trouble, diabetes, high blood pressure, one kidney removed, an arterial bypass, breast surgery, allergies (she met criteria #4 above quite well!) Not only that, but she left an air-conditioned house for one that wasn't, and broke out in terrible heat rashes, but the Hackberry group never knew it. Dr. Harvey bragged so on the biscuits and gravy she would cook for him, just like his mother used to. His 99-year-old mother is still living in 1986.

Dear children of Hackberry,

I hated not getting to see you all again, but we came near my house on the way back from Newport, Rhode Island, so I just came on home. It was best for me because it is so hard to get from Tuscaloosa. I know that everyone had a delightful summer program at Hackberry. I missed you so much this summer, but my thoughts were with you. I hope you have been as you always were for me, and I am sure you were because you are such sweet children anyway. I guess this is the last week of your stay there, so I know you are all sad as you are each summer. Look forward to next summer and put into practice all you have learned. Marvin, I was so glad to know you came through the surgery just fine. Be good boys and girls and keep trying and you will be all right. Kay, when you see Karen tell her "Hey" for me and tell Beretta I hated not seeing her. Give your mothers my love and best wishes. I will be thinking of you often. Don't forget me and the good times we spent together those three summers. I will see you again next year, I hope.

Love always to everyone,
Grandma Madaris

I came to appreciate her more than ever when I realized that she went to work for the first time away from home past the age at which I retired, and she worked until the mandatory Civil Service retirement age, in schools anyway, of 65. She was already 70 then when the law passed. She didn't really want to quit even so. The cause of her leaving Hackberry after 3 summers still make me laugh. After that summer session, all seven of my living brothers, sisters, their spouses, and sixteen of Mama's grandchildren were all calling and writing to ask "What did you do to Mama?" Of course I played dumb which was always easy for me.

Not until fall registration, when we three—Gale, Jasper, and I—returned from lunch to 204 Graves, and no secretaries had returned, did I understand. Gale went on to her office, and Dr. Harvey turned to me, after he sat down in Rosemary Wright's chair and I in Barbara Howell's, saying, "I am so sorry about what happened to your Mother." I was about to faint because I figured a call had come to the office before lunch that she was dead or sick, and he thought I might take it better on a full stomach. I looked at him not able to say a word; presumably he could tell I was confused. Twelve years of practice had made him an expert at this. He said, "I mean the green stamps," creating worse confusion than ever. I said, "What do you mean?" I knew later that he wished the campus had spread gossip faster and that I had heard because I suspect this great man had one of his most embarrassing moments. Gale came out of her office to help him out and to clasp her hand over my month when I burst out laughing.

It seemed that Wilson, the doctoral student director of Hackberry, had told Mama to keep the green stamps from the grocery buying each of the first two summers since she got such a small salary and worked long hours. In a way, you could say I got the green stamps, because Mama used them for her children's Christmas gifts. But this third summer of discontent, with federal grant money declining, one of the doctoral student professionals who also worked with the project—but not 24 hours a day like Mama did—decided the green stamps should be shared equally. I think it nearly broke up the department but finally the "yea's" must have won. The "nay's" may even have won but my mother, who took after her daughter, got so mad that she threw all the green stamps down on the table and refused to touch another one. Later, after going a safe distance away from Tuscaloosa—so she wouldn't spit on him, or worse—she wrote that dear, sweet department chairman. Dr. Harvey let me read it. He was my boss! She didn't even seem to care if I got fired! Mama and I never discussed it. She told him, among other things, that she intended to save up all her remaining green stamps forever after until she repaid all those she had unlawfully used the first two summers. I'll just bet she did too. No wonder I got no more expensive Christmas gifts! Today I feel certain Jasper and Mama have reconciled (in heaven, or wherever they are) but I still hope nobody gives out green stamps there.

I fully meant to head my list of suggestions for residential programs in SPE with the beginning suggestion (when I write my book), "Be sure to arrive at policies concerning the distribution of green stamps before any other decisions are made."

It's no wonder I still confuse the check-out girls when they give me my green stamps and I laugh uncontrolably. Am I glad Mental Retardation didn't have to deal with stamps! Dr. Elliott, if you come across a file full of green stamps someday, remember they are rightfully mine, as the next-of-kin!

It was a real joy to see those two "enemies" embrace like long-lost sweethearts at Los Angeles CEC banquet. Mama and Ben went because Mama had a married granddaughter there who had lived a military career life with her parents, and Mama didn't get to see her often. They stayed with her and did sight-seeing—Disney World, Knotts Berry Farm, all around—while I attended meetings. Mama had never gotten to do much traveling until her family was grown. She loved it!

I don't really feel that Dr. Harvey, or any of my later bosses, realized how those University students took advantage of me. At the Chicago CEC convention, nothing would do but for them to take me to a popular play, in between speeches, of course. They were very disappointed that no seats were available near any of them, expecially after they had all pooled their money to take me. I assured them I would be safe and would not get lost. Before the play started, people kept stopping, smiling, and passing their programs down the row for an autograph. The first time this happened, I smiled back, wondering who knew about an insignificant teacher from Alabama until the fellow next to me reached out and took the program just in time. It was intermission before I realized that I was sitting beside professional baseball player Ernie Banks, of the Chicago Cubs. He helped me with my coat at the conclusion, and I still have the coat! There were other times also when I was so glad to be sitting between total strangers. Later, Lila Niles White tried to explain it to me, but protesting the Vietnam war never did make sense to me! I can just remember the barefooted young folks sitting on the edge of the stage, plucking petals from a daisy. Upon returning home, my teenage children had one of their most embarrassing moments. It was not that I had attended the play, but that I had gone not knowing to what I was being taken. The play was "Hair". When does a special education teacher have time to read modern play reviews?

"I wish there were just something left these days that could honestly be called unmentionable"
—**Lark Bragg**

Speaking of CEC Conventions, I was a very capable chaperone—at least for the students; I didn't even attempt it with faculty! Dr. Harvey felt it necessary, however to draw up some rather specific rules for conduct. Actually, he borrowed it from the Knoxville '84 conference handbook sponsored by the General Department of Youth of the Wesleyan Church, page 9, with a few words changed.

Official Convention Rules
1. Obey all rules.
2. Always obey Rule #1.
3. No spitting on the floor.
4. Do everything you are told to do.
5. Do not throw food.
6. If arrested, don't mention The University of Alabama.
7. Anything else you shouldn't do, don't.

Each semester prior to student teaching, groups were brought together to file an application and, as the groups grew larger, some of the personal contact was lost, so attempts were made to get to know them and to place them with a teacher who might bring out the best in each one. Following the first seminar in the fall, one student waited after class to ask, "What do you mean by this?" pointing to a handwritten notation on her application for student teaching. Earlier, Dr. Don Crump, a co-worker whose judgement I had come to trust, had said, "Watch this one." What had I done but pencil in that statement on the application, adding the name of Dr. Crump? According to him, the student had stated that she had no intention of teaching, so she likely had little motivation. There was the card, back in the student's hands with that sentence which was meant to be erased before it was filed. Having innocently given them back for some other little bit of information, I had earnest desire for Graves 103 to open its trap door and plunge me to the basement. I didn't attempt to explain, feeling sure Don had discussed it with her previously and I assured her that what she did under my supervision would determine our relationship. It must have been good motivation, because she did a good job, and showed potential for making a good teacher, if she changed her mind. I soon retired, afraid I might do something else that stupid.

Howard Hinesley was an early student in special education classes, being a PE major and taking SPE only as an elective. He tells of a day that a 10-year-old student, Jackie, told him, "I brought my daddy's gun to school and I'm going to git Jim on the way home." Howard ignored the boy's threat at first but decided he had better tell the principal, and Mrs. McRimmon thought it best to let a policeman know. He came and found a loaded pistol under the shrubbery.

Each year the special ed wing held a Halloween Carnival to which the entire school was invited, and one year Howard's physically handicapped class had the haunted house. His mother-in-law was the fortune-teller, and Susan, his wife, was the body in the casket. A second grader came in and a student, Jimmy Osmore, was under the table to rub a cold hand on each leg as they passed; the teacher nearly trampled her class when this happened to her.

Howard learned what a good job he had done in teaching a unit on "The Human Body" when one boy stayed longer than usual in the bathroom. Howard went to check on him, and found him crying, "I caught my kidney in my zipper," the boy replied. Another time a boy named Pat Sailors had gone to collect and empty garbage cans from all the SPE wing after lunch. He, too, stayed longer than usual so again the teacher went to check on him. There he was, inside the dumpster, where the weight of the garbage in a can had caused him to lose his balance as he leaned over to empty it. Lunchroom scraps had just been put in the dumpster. As Howard leaned over to pull Pat out, he too fell in, wearing his best suit in anticipation of an important meeting. How would I have liked to see that! I'll bet it was a first for Northington.

Howard organized the first boy Scout troop for SPE class members there and it was very sucessful. I have a slide of the entire table-top community his class made, complete with power poles and wires. I knew he would someday get to be the assistant superintendent of a fine school system like that of Brevard County, Florida.

Grading

Twice in all those years I changed an internship grade upon request, and three times I refused; all the others were "final." The first two grades were felt to be misjudgements, with too many comparisons having been made with others in the group, these two students being the only males in classes of females. Upon hearing that one grade in that first semester of federal grant master's level students had been upped by one letter, a second one came with the same story, "Your grade kept me from making the Dean's list." Trying not to show partiality, I requested time to review my evaluation tools and stated that I would give consideration to the question. A look at the student's other grades for the semester revealed mostly C's, and the grade remained. When she returned for an A, I simply said, "There will be no change of grade. Your record showed no possibility of making Dean's List." "Do you mean you didn't trust me enough that you checked my grades in record's office?" "Should I have?" was the reply. The grade should have been changed, down rather than up. That student never listed me as a reference. How fortunate!

The other two grades not changed upon request were, first, the grade earned by the girl friend of someone's favorite student. That had never been a part of our evaluation criteria. She came to Verner late nearly every day, and got by with as little work as possible, thinking that she had it made. The second student to unsuccessfully petition for a higher grade, was a football player, the only one ever enrolled in any of my classes. I knew Bear Bryant expected a lot from his players, disciplined them, and let them know that he meant what he said. In fact, the Bear and I had a lot of the same philosophy. When this boy found it hard to make an 8:00 class, to show up for his practicum experience in physical education at Verner, or when he failed his tests, and didn't turn in his assignments, the proper form was filled out at mid-term stating that unsatisfactory work was endangering the student's credit for the course. Some advice by his counselor brought about reasonable results, but not enough, and there was no hope for a grade which would help him to keep a football scholarship. He pleaded, begged, and tried hard to do a semester's work in one day, but without success. He enrolled for spring semester again in the same SPE 96; his grade: ditto. He had apparently elected the course because word had gotten around that it was easy. Again, a look at the records indicated that other instructors besides me were responsible for his not being able to return. He was a likable, capable boy, but football players need to learn the facts of life, too.

There was also the new faculty member who said, "I have been asked to help draw up an adequate evaluation form for student teaching since the department never has had one." You don't question what doctors say, so I helped, thinking maybe some new criteria had been unearthed in recent times in some dissertation. After working on the committee hours on end all semester to come up with an adequate evaluation sheet, we came up with exactly what cooperating teachers and faculty supervisors had each been filing for every student teacher in the area of mental retardation since the summer of 1962.

Speaking of grading, Hanna Gillion asked me one day at the swimming pool, "Is it true that you only have one criterion for grading? Students tell me that if one is known to drink he fails; if he or she is a teetotaler, they get an A." My only reply was, "Then I am the highest over-grader in this whole university." Hanna never could tell truth from fiction, as revealed here. This was her "tribute" at the time of my retirement. (I can't wait till she retires):

"To set pen on paper and come up with an adequate description of Daisy Styles' personal and professional accomplishments would defy even the greatest among us. Many of her colleagues have already tried. I feel duty-bound to relate little known anecdotes that may otherwise be lost forever.

"Our professional relationship goes back further than either of us would elect to divulge. Suffice it to say though that SPE was still in the embryo stage. Martha Tack was a cute little red-headed girl running around the streets of Montgomery playing pranks. Paul Orr was in elementary school trying to learn not to dangle a participle. David Matthews was in Grove Hill having visions of being HEW Secretary. Tommy Russell was fightin' kudzu in Duncanville, and everybody was calling everybody else idiot, moron and/or imbecile.

"In the beginning—no reference to Genesis—no one would admit to being retarded. Daisy, in her usual proficient manner, set about appointing people to this category. SPE was alive and well and residing mostly in Barnwell Hall swimming pool. Those children were the cleanest, the best "swum," and the most supervised children ever seen before or since. There were twenty-nine interns to every child; sometimes we would get the interns confused with the children and give them swimming lessons. One of the children of the group was affected with narcolepsy, which heralded the beginning of the M & M therapy. He was so bad, so loud, so uncontrollable, and so obnoxious that we encouraged his having a seizure as that was the only time he was quiet. When he did, we gave him one M & M. His name was Ben.

"That was the infamous summer that the learned teacher put the Saran Wrap on the Elmer's glue and was completely unable to get glue out of the bottle for three weeks. One of the six-year olds from the trainable group finally came to her rescue by removing the Saran Wrap from the top.

"At this time in her career, Daisy Styles perfected the educational philosophy that if a teacher tried to talk louder than the students all would be lost. As a consequence, she has never spoken above a whisper and all the students learned to read lips because they thought she was mute.

"In an effort to teach social amenities, she always had the children make me 'something' in arts and crafts. I finally learned never to name anything I was given. I'd just say 'thank you so much for the _____' and look at her and she would mouth the name of the object. I learned to read her lips a little quicker than some of the children. To date I still have the momentos of my summer of discontent. Numbered among them are: a three-legged fertility doll, a severly tilted ash tray that won't hold one ash; a drawing of me in a black bathing suit that looks like an elephant lying down, and a genuine stick.

"The second summer we were unable to get even one child to play with. George Wallace had decided to stand in the school house door and the parents refused to let their children be a party to such a thing. A frantic plea was sent to Partlow. They replied, bussing us eight profoundly retarded children and one completely normal child. The eight profoundly retarded children we worked with beautifully but we were at a loss to deal with the normal child. We kept holding him by the hand and leading him places he didn't want to go!

"One of the children who was not known to be epileptic, but was, had a seizure in the water. No one was aware of the occurrence but me and as I hit the water I screamed, 'Mrs. Styles!' When I came up with the child there were forty-seven arms trying to get me out of the water. I later found out she had thought I was the one with the seizure because I had turned ashen. (Hanna didn't listen when I told her the first day that the child had seizures).

"One of the most profoundly retarded of that group, and one of the most beautiful children we have ever had, was named Roger. He would get a daily letter from his mother which Daisy would read to him. She would read a sentence and cry a sentence. It cost the University $103 worth of toilet paper that one summer because she kept blowing her nose. This child could not accept the fact that water would ruin his letter. Daisy finally convinced him that she could be responsible and hold it while he swam. Each time he turned in her direction she waved the letter like she was launching a fleet of jet planes. I was more professional than she was and was never emotionally affected by the child. For some reason though I always found it necessary to check the 'CROX' in the water so he would go swimming. Roger did a good job with us that summer.

"At times when we got bored—I remember one time in all those years—we would play games with each other, and one of our favorites was 'spot the other one's pet.' She always won hands down because she used the process of elimination. Mine was always the most cantankerous of the bunch. One child in particular still haunts us both. Each morning when she arrived at school her index finger would be mired in her navel. We began with textbook treatments of the problem. We said things like 'Why do you have your finger in your navel?' 'Wouldn't you like to point your finger at something?' To all of these she answered absolutely nothing. Finally, in desperation, we tried the direct approach: we ordered her to get her finger out of her navel—to which she again failed to reply. Finally one of the interns solved the problem and was convinced that the child thought her navel was her switch and she was turning herself on every morning. After that we encouraged her at every opportunity, but it short circuited. At first I was the only one who could 'handle' this particular child. It was not that I knew so much more than the others present or any of the other things one might suspect from a professional education point of view; it was just that I was the only one fleet of foot enough to catch her and strong enough to pick her up and put her where we wanted her to go.

Many more anecdotes could and probably should be written so that the neophyte could profit from the vast accumulation of knowledge of Daisy Styles. It will, however, forever remain unwritten because we might all get arrested for child abuse. As a closing tribute, though, I offer two things as testimony to her talent:

"1. She's one of the few people I've ever met who managed to stay on a diet all her life while never losing a pound, and, "2. A student of mine said to me once that the second retarded group was much more difficult to control and teach than the first. When I asked what second retarded group, he said the one that came at 9:10. It took me three days to muster enough courage to tell him that the group he was talking about was a 'normal' fourth grade class. Daisy's group was first."

—Hanna Gillion

Hanna has told you something of that summer of 1963, a time when our first black student enrolled at the University. We did have to seek students, as many did not come because they were afraid there would be trouble on campus. Our group was composed largely of Partlow residents since the state delighted in getting some of the residents out in public schools. There was no trouble at all.

When forewarning came the next summer of a black student teacher being scheduled to teach white children in Special Education, Mrs. Mildred Grant who was principal of Verner School, training school of the College of Education called Dr. Harvey and me in and requested that we move our class to Graves Hall. She felt sure many parents of regular classes would withdraw their children, and we agreed to this, but as time passed my thinking changed and I kept the class at Verner. After all, University movers would not be very happy to be called to move back all my worldly goods when they had just carted them over from a third floor Graves Hall attic. Days had been spent setting up the classroom, and even the bulletin boards were ready. There came a time when I said, "Please, let's give it a try and we'll move at the first hint of any trouble; however, I don't believe there will be any." The peer group interaction would all be missing, there would be no playground, and also those teachers were going back in the fall to the public schools, not to the ivy halls of a sheltered college campus with no problems. By then, Dr. Harvey had learned not to cross me and had learned that I could throw temper tantrums or shed tears. So it was with reluctance that everybody appeared on opening day of summer school, holding his or her breath. At least now there would be fifteen pupils and fifteen interns to help move if it became necessary.

Not one thing changed at Verner. In fact, I remember it as one of my most delightful summers. I can still see Dianne sitting on the lap of one of our black student teachers, while she read the group a story, gently stroking the pretty gray hair that had a texture different from her own. How much we learned that summer! Those black teachers, by their own choice, led many seminars on how to deal with the common differences among many white and black children.

What fun it was ordering materials that first spring of 1962. I had never had so much before. There were whole sets of books and literally anything my heart desired. That was the first time I used the "Cowboy Sam" series from Benefic Press. I have had a sneaky feeling many times since that whatever couldn't be bought under federal grants could be covered by Jasper Harvey grants—straight from his billfold. Too, I used all my own children's books. I still have some with SPE stamped on them. An overzealous committee of school children stamped all of my books one summer along with those of the Department!

After school one day, down to the University I drove to pick up the first shipment. I wanted to try them out a little before school was out, since the same students would be using them in summer school. When Dr. Harvey began talking of long-range plans as he helped me take them to my car, I just couldn't let him go on any more, so I broke my secrecy rule. "The doctor has just told me I am pregnant so I can't promise anything beyond this summer." This was the most profound statement I have ever made, and can anybody guess what a choice Texas-language welcome Dr. Harvey gave this new little blessing? You're right. George and I had already decided my teaching career was about to end because I had let the other two grow up as best they could. Besides, his principal's salary had now reached $485 for each of twelve months. My first year in Tuscaloosa County was at the rate of $80 for seven months. George was teaching in high school, so he did get $85 for nine months. Dr. Harvey relented a little and erased my tears by saying, "He will be a lucky baby".

Dr. Harvey kept the secret though, because we didn't tell Mama until Mother's Day when I wrote on her card, "Why did you have to set your children such a good example?" Next day I followed it with a letter telling everything. She had her ninth and final child in 1939 when I was a senior in college and she was also in her forties. She had scattered them, one every two years, and stayed in practice. She never knew I told Dr. Harvey first.

We told the teachers at Cottondale the last day of school. George put a note in each box, "Thanks for your support of the recent 5-mil tax for the city of Tuscaloosa, earmarked for schools. We didn't think we would benefit directly from it but it seems we will. Watch for the lastest Styles in the fall." We refrained from telling people and nobody else told either, and I wondered later if anybody believed it. In summer school I dealt with fifteen children, fifteen interns, a school principal, ten co-teachers, a retarded janitor, and Hanna Gillion, and yet word didn't leak out till about the Fourth of July. I knew something was wrong when they suddenly would offer to perform tasks, like opening the windows, or lifting boxes, which I had been doing all summer. Then came the party, and the gift of a little silver spoon—engraved SPE 207 - 1962—tied with a blue ribbon around the neck of a white rubber lamb. The spoon, and a treasured fork from Alpha Brown, are in a safe place with which Ben is familiar. The blue bunting that the Harvey's bought was handed down to my nephew in Texas, but we still have a battery-operated race car set, a GI Joe for which we bought a sidecar motorcycle, plus a beautiful coral colored nylon gown, worn for the first time on November 14, 1962, and which I am still wearing. The gown will go in my archives with the coat to the suit I made to wear to the AEA Convention on March 13, 1962, when I stood as President of the State Teachers of Exceptional Children. The dress was printed brown silk with a reversible beige coat, lined with the same dress material, and I wore a fancy brown and beige hat with a veil and flowers. I couldn't find the material I wanted for the coat, so I finally settled on some upholstery material, purposely using the wrong side, which was prettier. When I modeled it for George he said, "You have made yourself a maternity coat!" Of course I laughed, but not for very long.

Ben got even with Dr. Harvey for that happy welcome; I can still see the look on Jasper's face when Ben about the age two or three, at our door, refused to get in his car. Finally, Jasper and the couple of students unloaded and got in my car with me driving. I guess we were going to a school nearby, maybe in Pickens County, and they needed me to show them the way. Ben had gone through some kind of trauma a couple of days before when Geneva Folsom had taken a turn driving my car with Ben along, and he yelled like he would die. I guess he had learned that his mother's driving could be depended on, but he wasn't too sure of other people. He got over it after that and doesn't show any real side effects now. Strangely, neither son can bear to ride with parental drivers today. They bribe us to let them drive, even though we remind them we have been at it for more than 100 years between us and never had a wreck. I guess they think the law of averages is about to run out.

Rob Kulbedia understood perfectly my boys not wanting to ride with me after a certain day when I was the lead car in a "funeral" procession of all student teachers and their classes for a picnic at Hurricane Creek. We lost his carload of children. Finally, I went back and found them seeing the sights of Holt. He declared he couldn't keep up with me! Of course I was familiar with the crooks and turns, and told him you never would get there if you didn't drive the speed limit. You know I'm a good driver; otherwise, Dr. Heller wouldn't have let me drive a University car packed full of his students—maybe not his favorite ones—to CEC in Washington, D.C. He did let me fly to Toronto, however.

Another memorable occasion was near the time of Mrs. Alpha Brown's retirement in 1969, when Dr. and Mrs. Harvey invited all the faculty for dinner. It was a delightfull occasion, except for the little family dog that barked pitifully, shut up in a room, when he was accustomed to being one of the family. The one fact I can reall from "Speech Problems of Exceptional Children" was that dogs can hear tones with much higher frequencies than people. Also, at the end of the main course when Dr. Harvey was helping Kathryn remove food as she was bringing in dessert, their signals backfired and cake flew in every direction, but I don't recall any broken dishes. Dr. Harvey was totally speechless. Can you imagine that? Nobody laughed. I'm so glad it didn't happen as the food was being served!

One anecdote I shall never forget, told to me by Doris Patterson, concerns a time Dr. Harvey saw fit to change his lectures somewhat because of two Catholic sisters enrolled in the days when habits were still worn. One week during their absence he let "his hair down". Upon their return they remained after class to see him, and he cringed since he knew they had heard of his teaching the week before. They had come to complain about the way in which he had shown discrimination. For the remainder of the course, he was his usual self.

April 14, 1975

My final student teaching seminar met at Cottondale School in Judy Blanton's classroom. We rotated locations quite often so that they would all have the opportunity to see as many settings as possible. Judy was very creative and had created many excellent teaching aids. Being an airline stewardess must be a pretty good background for special education. Going into her classroom always brought to mind the day when I happened to be there to witness a most unusual experience—the only one of its kind. Judy was pale, in a state of shock, deeply distressed, and I could just imagine that some terrible, traumatic experience had befallen her. When she got around to sharing with me the cause of her condition, she opened the closet door and let me see a cage where her hamster—which she had assumed was a male—had all morning been giving birth to 15 babies. Her pupils had been intrigued for awhile, but when Judy could stand it no longer she put the animals in solitary confinement. She declared they were premature, and I saw no point in arguing with her. She had succeeded in getting the children's minds, if not her own mind, on something else. My visit had to be cut short so that I could laugh all the way to the next school. When I see her again, I must remember to ask if she still raises hamsters. Probably so, because she's now the teacher of the academically gifted in Selma. I hear that she has a retired doctor friend who fascinates her class by coming and talking with them. It would not surprise me if she has him there just in case more hamsters arrive prematurely.

So much remains to be told. The last three years, teaching was year-round with some delightful interim couses including a camping course in which every member of my family assisted. There was the day the train wrecked at Coaling and several of the girls' best friends were on it, so they would not leave Tuscaloosa until they knew the results. The Walker County group joining us at Wolf Creek had supper ready when we arrived. What fun we had that night singing around the campfire! But the next day it was back to the salt mines. For the remainder of the course we looked at practical aspects of our work and dabbled in everything we could think of in that category, from driver training to greenhousery. It was hard to explain to the Interim Committee that these were worthwhile. It's what club women and senior citizens do all the time.

This letter which came following an interim course made all my teaching wothwhile:

Dear Mrs. Styles,

I forgot to leave these books with you at the completion of our workshop in Jasper. Thank you for letting us use them, and I hope you have not needed them.

I want to thank you for the wonderful experience I had at Wolf Creek. Besides learning so many useful things in Arts and Crafts, I feel that I have gotten a good course in "human development". Being around you with your kind, soothing ways, your positive attitude toward people (including your family), and your constant smile and gentleness, has made me realize what it takes to make children enjoy and look forward to the next day of life.

Thank you for a course that will help me be a better teacher the rest of my life. I mean all these things from my heart.

Sincerely,
Sara Strong

As I close this endeavor, which has been a pleasure from the day it was first planned, may I use words from Dr. Harvey's teacher, Dr. Bill Wolfe, as he spoke to our department in 103 Graves Hall in the early days of teacher-training in the field of Special Education:

> Now I get me up to work,
> I pray the Lord I will not shirk.
> If I should die before the night,
> I pray the Lord my work's all right.

Glossary

Ataxic cerebral palsy - a form of cerebral palsy marked by poor coordination in voluntary muscular movements.

Athetosis (athetoid) - involuntary purposeless movement of limbs caused by cerebral palsy, encephalitis, and tabes dorsalis.

Cerebral palsy - any one of a group of conditions affecting control of the motor system due to lesions (damage) in various parts of the brain.

Educable mentally retarded (EMR) - a degree of mental retardation where often the child is only retarded in school. Their social and communication skills are frequently normal or nearly so. They are likely to become independent or semi-independent adults. Most generally master standard academic skills up to about the sixth grade level. IQs range from 50-75.

Epilepsy - the name given to a group of nervous diseases marked primarily by convulsions of varying forms and degrees.

Exceptional people - those whose performance deviates (differs) from normal people, either below or above, to the extent that special education is needed or desirable.

Gran mal seizures - an epileptic seizure in which the convulsions are severe and widespread with long loss of awareness.

Hydrocephalus - a condition of excess cerebrospinal fluid within the brain which causes mental retardation. Can be helped with a shunt operation.

Learning disabilities - a disorder in one or more of the basic psychological processes involved in understanding or in using spoken or written language which causes difficulty in listening, thinking, speaking, reading, writing, spelling, or to do mathematical calculations.

Mental retardation - refers to significantly subaverage general intellectual functioning existing concurrently with deficits in adaptive behavior and manifested during the developmental period.

Multi-handicapped - a condition with two or more disabilities that prevents normal development, such as cerebral palsy and mental retardation or blind and physically handicapped. Most require use of crutches, wheelchairs, or other adaptive devices for mobility and learning.

Neurologically impaired - pertains to any abnormal function of the nervous system.

Orthopedically impaired - any involvement that limits the motor activity of the student.

Paraplegic - paralysis of the legs and lower part of the body, both motion and sensation being affected.

Petit mal seizures - epileptic seizures in which there may be only a momentary dizziness or blackout or some automatic action of which the patient has no knowledge.

Phenylketonuria (PKU) - an inherited metabolic disease which can cause severe retardation. Can now be detected at birth and the bad effects prevented with a special diet.

Retrolental fibroplasia - a condition characterized by abnormally dense growth of blood vessels and scar tissue in the eye, often causing total blindness.

Special class - a special education administrative arrangement which has a small teacher-pupil ratio in which children are placed based on their disability. The teacher has specialized training in instructing children with a specific disability such as mental retardation, blind, deaf, etc.

Special education - the individually planned and systematically monitored arrangement of physical setting, special equipment, materials, and teaching procedures for education purposes.

Trainable - a degree of mental retardation that is shown early in life. Most will require life-long supervision but can live in the community-based residences and work in supervised settings. IQ range is from 30-50 on a standardized test.